Gold-digging Ants

Ancient Egypt, *c.* 415 BC

HERODOTUS

Snakes with Wings and Gold-digging Ants

Translated by AUBREY DE SELINCOURT
Translation revised by JOHN MARINCOLA

GREAT
JOURNEYS

PENGUIN BOOKS

Published by the Penguin Group
Penguin Books Ltd, 80 Strand, London WC2R ORL, England
Penguin Group (USA) Inc., 375 Hudson Street, New York, New York 10014, USA
Penguin Group (Canada), 90 Eglinton Avenue East, Suite 700, Toronto, Ontario, Canada M4P 2Y3
(a division of Pearson Penguin Canada Inc.)
Penguin Ireland, 25 St Stephen's Green, Dublin 2, Ireland (a division of Penguin Books Ltd)
Penguin Group (Australia), 250 Camberwell Road, Camberwell, Victoria 3124, Australia
(a division of Pearson Australia Group Pty Ltd)
Penguin Books India Pvt Ltd, 11 Community Centre, Panchsheel Park, New Delhi – 110 017, India
Penguin Group (NZ), 67 Apollo Drive, Mairangi Bay, Auckland 1310, New Zealand
(a division of Pearson New Zealand Ltd)
Penguin Books (South Africa) (Pty) Ltd, 24 Sturdee Avenue, Rosebank, Johannesburg 2196, South Africa

Penguin Books Ltd, Registered Offices: 80 Strand, London WC2R ORL, England

www.penguin.com

The Histories first published in Penguin Classics 1954
This extract published in Penguin Books 2007
1

Translation copyright © Aubrey de Selincourt, 1954
Revised translation copyright © John Marincola, 1996, 2003
All rights reserved

The moral right of the translator has been asserted

Inside-cover maps by Jeff Edwards

Taken from the Penguin Classics edition of The Histories,
translated by Aubrey de Selincourt, revised by John Marincola

Typeset by Rowland Phototypesetting Ltd, Bury St Edmunds, Suffolk
Printed in England by Clays Ltd, St Ives plc

ISBN: 978-0-141-02533-9

Contents

Exiled from Helicarnassus after his involvement in an unsuccessful coup d'état against the ruling dynasty, Herodotus (*c.* 490–415 BC) undertook some of the many journeys described in his *Histories*. His reputation has varied greatly, but he is often still known by the title, first given to him by Cicero, of the 'Father of History'.

Vessels of Silver and the Headless Corpse

There are not a great many wild animals in Egypt, in spite of the fact that it borders on Libya. Such as there are – both wild and tame – are without exception held to be sacred.

[...]

The various sorts have guardians appointed for them, sometimes men, sometimes women, who are responsible for feeding them; and the office of guardian is handed down from father to child. Their manner, in the various cities, of performing vows is as follows: praying to the god to whom the particular creature, whichever it may be, is sacred, they shave the heads of their children – sometimes completely, sometimes only a half or a third part – and after weighing the hair in a pair of scales, give an equal weight of silver to the animals' keeper, who then cuts up fish (the animals' usual food) to an equivalent value and gives it to the animal to eat. Anyone who deliberately kills one of these animals, is punished with death; should one be killed accidentally, the penalty is whatever the priests choose to impose; but for killing an ibis or a hawk, whether deliberately or not, the penalty is inevitably death.

The number, already large, of domestic animals would have been greatly increased, were it not for an odd thing that happens to the cats. The females, when they have kittens, avoid the toms; but the toms, thus deprived of their satisfaction, get over the difficulty very ingeniously, for they either openly seize, or secretly steal, the kittens and kill them – but without eating them – and the result is that the females, deprived of their kittens and wanting more (for their maternal instinct is very strong), go off to look for mates again. What happens when a house catches fire is most extra-ordinary: nobody takes the least trouble to put it out, for it is only the cats that matter: everyone stands in a row, a little distance from his neighbour, trying to protect the cats, who nevertheless slip through the line, or jump over it, and hurl themselves into the flames. This causes the Egyptians deep distress. All the in-mates of a house where a cat has died a natural death shave their eyebrows, and when a dog dies they shave the whole body including the head. Cats which have died are taken to Bubastis, where they are embalmed and buried in sacred receptacles; dogs are buried, also in sacred burial-places, in the towns where they be-long. Mongooses are buried in the same way as dogs; field-mice and hawks are taken to Buto, ibises to Hermopolis. Bears, which are scarce, and wolves (which in Egypt are not much bigger than foxes) are buried wherever they happen to be found lying dead.

The following is an account of the crocodile. During the four winter months it takes no food. It is a four-footed, amphibious creature, lays and hatches its eggs on land, where it spends the greater part of the day, and stays all night in the river, where the water is warmer than the night-air and the dew. The difference in size between the young and the full-grown crocodile is greater than in any other known creature; for a crocodile's egg is hardly bigger than a goose's, and the young when hatched is small in proportion, yet it grows to a size of some twenty-three feet long or even more. It has eyes like a pig's but great fang-like teeth in proportion to its body, and is the only animal to have no tongue and a stationary lower jaw; for when it eats it brings the upper jaw down upon the under. It has powerful claws and a scaly hide, which on its back is impenetrable. It cannot see under water, though on land its sight is remarkably sharp. One result of its spending so much time in the water is that the inside of its mouth gets covered with leeches. Other animals avoid the crocodile, as do all birds too with one exception – the sandpiper, or Egyptian plover; this bird is of service to the crocodile and lives, in consequence, in the greatest amity with him; for when the crocodile comes ashore and lies with his mouth wide open (which he generally does facing towards the west), the bird hops in and swallows the leeches. The crocodile enjoys this, and never, in consequence, hurts the bird. Some Egyptians reverence the crocodile as a sacred beast; others do not, but treat it as an enemy. The strongest belief in its sanctity is to be found in Thebes and round about Lake Moeris; in these places they keep one particular crocodile, which they tame, putting rings made of glass or gold into its ears and bracelets round its front feet, and giving it special food and ceremonial offerings. In fact, while these creatures are alive they treat them with every kindness, and, when they die, embalm them and bury them in sacred tombs. On the other hand, in the neighbourhood of Elephantine crocodiles are not considered sacred animals at all, but are eaten. In the Egyptian language these creatures are called *champsae*. The name crocodile – or 'lizard' – was given them by the Ionians, who saw they resembled the lizards commonly found on stone walls in their own country.

Of the numerous different ways of catching crocodiles I will describe the one which seems to me the most worthy to report. They bait a hook with a chine of pork and let it float out into midstream, and at the same time, standing on the bank, take a live pig and beat it. The crocodile, hearing its squeals, makes a rush towards it, encounters the bait, gulps it down, and is hauled out of the water. The first thing the huntsman does when he has got the beast on land is to plaster its eyes with mud; this done, it is dispatched easily enough – but without this precaution it will give a lot of trouble.

The hippopotamus is held sacred in the district of Papremis, but not elsewhere. This animal has four legs, cloven hoofs like an ox, a snub nose, a horse's mane and tail, conspicuous tusks, a voice like a horse's neigh, and is about the size of a very large ox. Its hide is so thick and tough that when dried it can be made into spear-shafts. Otters, too, are found in the Nile; they, and the fish called lepidotus, and eels are all considered sacred to the Nile, as is also the bird known as the fox-goose. Another sacred bird is the phoenix; I have not seen a phoenix myself, except in paintings, for it is very rare and visits the country (so they say at Heliopolis) only at intervals of 500 years, on the occasion of the death of the parent-bird. To judge by the paintings, its plumage is partly golden, partly red, and in shape and size it is exactly like an eagle. There is a story about the phoenix which I do not find credible; it brings its parent in a lump of myrrh all the way from Arabia and buries the body in the temple of the Sun. To perform this feat, the bird first shapes some myrrh into a sort of egg as big as it finds, by testing, that it can carry; then it hollows the lump out, puts its father inside and smears some more myrrh over the hole. The egg-shaped lump is then just of the same weight as it was originally. Finally it is carried by the bird to the temple of the Sun in Egypt. Such, at least, is the story.

Near Thebes a species of snake is found said to be sacred to Zeus; these snakes are small and quite harmless, and have two horns growing from the top of their heads. Such as are found dead are buried in the temple of Zeus.

There is a place in Arabia more or less opposite the city of Buto, where I went to try to get information about the flying snakes. On my arrival I saw their skeletons in incalculable numbers; they were piled in heaps, some of which were big, others smaller, others smaller still, and there were many piles of them. The place where these bones lie is a narrow mountain pass leading to a broad plain which joins on to the plain of Egypt, and it is said that when the winged snakes fly to Egypt from Arabia in spring, the ibises meet them at the entrance to the pass and do not let them get through, but kill them. According to the Arabians, this service is the reason for the great reverence with which the ibis is regarded in Egypt, and the Egyptians themselves admit the truth of what they say. The ibis is jet-black all over; it has legs like a crane's, a markedly hooked beak, and is about the size of a crake. That, at any rate, is what the black ibis is like – the kind namely that attacks the winged snakes; there is, however, another sort, more commonly found in inhabited districts; this has a bald head and neck and is white except for the head, throat, wing-tips, and rump, which are jet-black; its legs and beak are similar to those of the black ibis. The winged snakes resemble watersnakes; their wings are not feathered, but are like a bat's. I will now leave the subject of sacred animals and say something of the people.

The Egyptians who live in the cultivated parts of the country, by their practice of keeping records of the past, have made themselves much the most learned of any nation of which I have had experience. I will describe some of their habits: every month for three successive days they purge themselves, for their health's sake, with emetics and clysters, in the belief that all diseases come from the food a man eats; and it is a fact – even apart from this precaution – that next to the Libyans they are the healthiest people in the world. I should put this down myself to the absence of changes in the climate; for change, and especially change of weather, is the prime cause of disease. They eat loaves made from emmer – *cyllestes* is their word for them – and drink a wine made from barley, as they have no vines in the country. Some kinds of fish they eat raw, either dried in the sun, or salted; quails, too, they eat raw, and ducks and various small birds, after pickling them in brine; other sorts of birds and fish, apart from those which they consider sacred, they either roast or boil. When the rich give a party and the meal is finished, a man carries round amongst the guests a wooden image of a corpse in a coffin, carved and painted to look as much like the real thing as possible, and anything from eighteen inches to three foot long; he shows it to each guest in turn, and says: 'Look upon this body as you drink and enjoy yourself; for you will be just like it when you are dead.'

The Egyptians keep to their native customs and never adopt any from abroad. Many of these customs are interesting, especially, perhaps, the 'Linus' song. This person, under different names, is celebrated in song not only in Egypt but in Phoenicia, Cyprus, and other places, and appears to be the person whom the Greeks celebrate as Linus; if this is so, it is yet one more of the many surprises that Egypt has to offer; for where did the Egyptians get this song from? It is clearly very ancient; the Egyptian name for Linus is Maneros, and their story is that their first king had an only son, who died young, and that this dirge – their first and only melody – was invented to be sung in his honour.

There is another point in which the Egyptians resemble one section of the Greek people – the Lacedaemonians: I mean the custom of young men stepping

7

aside to make room for their seniors when they meet them in the street, and of getting up from their seats when older men come in. But they are unlike any of the Greeks in that they do not greet one another by name in the streets, but make a low bow and drop one hand to the knee. The clothes they wear consist of a linen tunic with a fringe hanging round the legs (called in their language *calasiris*), and a white woollen garment on top of it. It is, however, contrary to religious usage to be buried in a woollen garment, or to wear wool in a temple. This custom agrees with the rites known as Orphic and Bacchic (actually Egyptian and Pythagorean); for anyone initiated into these rites is similarly debarred from burial in a garment of wool. They have a sacred story which explains the reason for this.

The Egyptians were also the first to assign each month and each day to a particular deity, and to foretell by the date of a man's birth his character, his fortunes, and the day of his death – a discovery which Greek poets have turned to account. The Egyptians, too, have made more use of omens and prognostics than any other nation; they keep written records of the observed results of any unusual phenomenon, so that they come to expect a similar consequence to follow a similar occurrence in the future. The art of divination is not attributed by them to any man, but only to certain gods: for instance, Heracles, Apollo, Athena, Artemis, Ares, and Zeus all have an oracle in the country, while the oracle of Leto in Buto is held in greater repute than any of them. The method of delivering the responses varies in the different shrines.

The practice of medicine they split up into separate parts, each doctor being responsible for the treatment of only one disease. There are, in consequence, innumerable doctors, some specializing in diseases of the eyes, others of the head, others of the teeth, others of the stomach, and so on; while others, again, deal with the sort of troubles which cannot be exactly localized. As regards mourning and funerals, when a distinguished man dies all the women of the household plaster their heads and faces with mud, then, leaving the body indoors, perambulate the town with the dead man's female relatives, their dresses fastened with a girdle, and beat their bared breasts. The men too, for their part, follow the same procedure, wearing a girdle and beating themselves like the women. The ceremony over, they take the body to be mummified.

Mummification is a distinct profession. The embalmers, when a body is brought to them, produce specimen models in wood, painted to resemble nature, and graded in quality; the best and most expensive kind is said to represent a being whose name I shrink from mentioning in this connexion; the next best is somewhat inferior and cheaper, while the third sort is cheapest of all. After pointing out these differences in quality, they ask which of the three is required, and the kinsmen of the dead man, having agreed upon a price, go away and leave the embalmers to their work. The most perfect process is as follows: as much as possible of the brain is extracted through the nostrils with an iron hook, and what the hook cannot reach is rinsed out with drugs; next the flank is laid open with a flint knife and the whole contents of the abdomen removed; the cavity is then thoroughly cleansed and washed out, first with palm wine and again with an infusion of pounded spices. After that it is filled with pure bruised myrrh, cassia, and every other aromatic substance with the exception of frankincense, and sewn up again, after which the body is placed in natrum, covered entirely over, for seventy days – never longer. When this period, which must not be exceeded, is over, the body is washed and then wrapped from head to foot in linen cut into strips and smeared on the under side with gum, which is commonly used by the Egyptians instead of glue. In this condition the body is given back to the family, who have a wooden case made, shaped like the human figure, into which it is put. The case is then sealed up and stored in a sepulchral chamber, upright against the wall. When, for reasons of expense, the second quality is called for, the treatment is different: no incision is made and the intestines are not removed, but oil of cedar is injected with a syringe into the body through the anus which is afterwards stopped up to prevent the liquid from escaping. The body is then pickled in natrum for the prescribed number of days, on the last of which the oil is drained off. The effect of it is so powerful that as it leaves the body it brings with it the stomach and intestines in a liquid state, and as the flesh, too, is dissolved by the natrum, nothing of the body is left but the bones and skin. After this treatment it is returned to the family without further fuss.

The third method, used for embalming the bodies

of the poor, is simply to clear out the intestines with a purge and keep the body seventy days in natrum. It is then given back to the family to be taken away.

When the wife of a distinguished man dies, or any woman who happens to be beautiful or well known, her body is not given to the embalmers immediately, but only after the lapse of three or four days. This is a precautionary measure to prevent the embalmers from violating the corpse, a thing which is said actually to have happened in the case of a woman who had just died. The culprit was given away by one of his fellow workmen. If anyone, either an Egyptian or a foreigner, is found drowned in the river or killed by a crocodile, there is the strongest obligation upon the people of the nearest town to have the body embalmed in the most elaborate manner and buried in a consecrated burial-place; no one is allowed to touch it except the priests of the Nile – not even relatives or friends; the priests alone prepare it for burial with their own hands and place it in the tomb, as if it were something more sacred than the body of a man.

The Egyptians are unwilling to adopt Greek customs, or, to speak generally, those of any other country. There is, however, one exception to this almost universal rule in the case of Chemmis, a large town near Neapolis in the district of Thebes. In this place there is a square of enclosed ground sacred to Perseus the son of Danae; palm trees grow round it, and there is a stone gateway of great size surmounted by two very large stone figures. Within the enclosure is a shrine containing a statue of Perseus. According to the people of Chemmis, Perseus is frequently to be seen in the neighbourhood, and also within the temple; sometimes a sandal which he has worn, three feet long, is found – a sign, they say, of the approach of a period of great prosperity for the whole of Egypt. In the worship of Perseus Greek ceremonies are used, athletic contests with all the usual events, and prizes of cattle, cloaks, and skins. When I asked why it was that Perseus revealed himself only to the people of Chemmis, and why they alone of the Egyptians celebrated games in his honour, the answer was that Perseus belonged by birth to their city; Danaus and Lynceus, they said, were Chemmies before they sailed to Greece, and from them they traced Perseus' descent. Further, when he came to Egypt from Libya with the Gorgon's head (which is the reason the Greeks also assign for his going there) he paid a visit to Chemmis, having previously learned the name of the place from his mother, and there acknowledged all his kinsmen. On his arrival he instructed them to celebrate games in his honour, and they accordingly did so.

Up to this point I have described the life of the Egyptians who live south of the marsh-country; those who inhabit the marshes are in most things much the same as the rest; and they also practise monogamy, as the Greeks do; nevertheless they are peculiar in certain ways which they have discovered of living more cheaply: for instance, they gather the water-lilies (called lotus by the Egyptians), which grow in great abundance when the river is full and floods the neighbouring flats, and dry them in the sun; then from the centre of each blossom they pick out something which resembles a poppy-head, grind it, and make it into loaves which they bake. The root of this plant is also edible; it is round, about as big as an apple, and tastes fairly sweet. There is another kind of lily to be found in the river; this resembles a rose, and its fruit is formed on a separate stalk from that which bears the blossom, and has very much the look of a wasps' comb. The fruit contains a number of seeds, about the size of an olive-stone, which are good to eat either fresh or dried. They pull up the annual crop of papyrus-reed which grows in the marshes, cut the stalks in two, and eat the lower part, about eighteen inches in length, first baking it in a closed pan, heated red-hot, if they want to enjoy it to perfection. They also sell it. The upper section of the stalk is used for some other purpose. Some of these people, however, live upon nothing but fish, which they gut as soon as they catch them, and eat after drying them in the sun.

Gregarious fish are not found in large numbers in the rivers; they frequent the lakes, which they leave at the breeding season to swim in shoals to the sea. In front go the males, dropping their milt, which the females, following behind, gulp down. It is this that causes the females to conceive, and after a period in the sea, when they are about to spawn, the whole shoal returns to its former haunt in the inland lakes. This time, however, it is the females who lead the way, and as they swim along in their hundreds they do just what the males did on the way out, dropping their grains of spawn, a little here, a little there, while the males who follow behind swallow them up. Each of these grains of spawn is a fish in embryo; some of them escape and are not swallowed by the males, and it is these which afterwards grow to maturity. Fish which are caught on their way to the sea are found to have their heads bruised on the left side, while those taken as they return upstream have similar bruises on the right side. The reason is that as they swim down river to the sea they keep close to the bank on their left, and still stick to the same side of the river on their return, keeping as near the bank as they possibly can and continually brushing against it, for fear of being carried out of their course by the strength of the stream.

When the Nile begins to rise, the hollows and marshy ground close beside it are the first to fill, the water from the river seeping through the banks, and no sooner are these low-lying bits of ground formed into lakes than they are found to contain a multitude of small fish. I think I understand the probable reason for this: the fish, I should say, when the river is falling the previous year, lay their eggs in the mud just before they get away with the last of the water, so that when the flood comes round again in due course, the eggs at once hatch and produce the fish. These are the facts about the fish in the Nile.

The Egyptians who live in the marsh-country use an oil extracted from the castor-oil plant. This plant, which grows wild in Greece, they call *Kiki*, and the Egyptian variety is very prolific and has a disagreeable smell. Their practice is to sow it along the banks of rivers and lakes, and when the fruit is gathered it is either cut and pressed, or else roasted and boiled down, and the liquid thus obtained is of an oily nature and quite as good as olive-oil for burning in lamps, though the smell is unpleasant.

The country is infested by swarms of mosquitoes, and the people have invented various methods of dealing with them; south of the marshes they sleep at night on raised structures, which is a great benefit to them because the mosquitoes are prevented by the wind from flying high; in the marsh-country itself they do not have these towers, but everyone, instead, provides himself with a net, which during the day he uses for fishing, and at night fixes up round his bed, and creeps in under it before he goes to sleep. For anyone to sleep wrapped in a cloak or in linen would be useless, for the mosquitoes would bite through them; but they do not even attempt to get through the net.

The Nile boats used for carrying freight are built of acacia wood – the acacia resembles in form the lotus of Cyrene, and exudes gum. They cut short planks, about three feet long, from this tree, and the method of construction is to lay them together like bricks and through-fasten them with dowels set close together, and then, when the hull is complete, to lay the benches across on top. The boats have no ribs and are caulked from inside with papyrus. They are given a single steering-oar, which is driven down through the keel; the masts are of acacia wood, the sails of papyrus. These vessels cannot sail up the river without a good leading wind, but have to be towed from the banks; and for dropping downstream with the current they are handled as follows: each vessel is equipped with a raft made of tamarisk wood, with a rush mat fastened on top of it, and a stone with a hole through it weighing some hundred pounds; the raft and the stone are made fast to the vessel with ropes, fore and aft respectively, so that the raft is carried rapidly forward by the current and pulls the 'baris' (as these boats are called) after it, while the stone, dragging along the bottom astern, acts as a check and gives her steerage-way. There are a great many of these vessels on the Nile, some of them of many tons' carrying capacity.

When the Nile overflows, the whole country is converted into a sea, and the towns, which alone remain above water, look like the islands in the Aegean. At these times water transport is used all over the country, instead of merely along the course of the river, and anyone going from Naucratis to Memphis would pass right by the pyramids instead of following the usual course by Cercasorus and the tip of the Delta. If you go by boat from Canopus on the coast across the flats to Naucratis, you will pass Anthylla and Archandropolis, of which the former, a city of some repute, has been made over ever since the Persian conquest of Egypt to the wife of the reigning monarch to keep her in shoes. The latter town, I fancy, took the name of Archandropolis from Archander the son of Phthius, grandson of Achaeus and son-in-law of Danaus. There may, of course, have been another Archander; but the name in any case is not Egyptian.

Up to this point I have confined what I have written to the results of my own direct observation and research, and the views I have formed from them; but from now on the basis of my story will be the accounts given to me by the Egyptians themselves – though here, too, I shall put in one or two things which I have seen with my own eyes.

The priests told me that it was Min, the first king of Egypt, who raised the dam which created Memphis. The river used to flow along the base of the sandy hills on the Libyan border, and this monarch, by damming it up at the bend about a hundred furlongs south of Memphis, drained the original channel and diverted it to a new one half-way between the two lines of hills. To this day the elbow which the Nile forms here, where it is forced into its new channel, is most carefully watched by the Persians, who strengthen the dam every year; for should the river burst it, Memphis might be completely overwhelmed. On the land which had been drained by the diversion of the river, King Min built the city which is now called Memphis – it lies in the narrow part of Egypt – and afterwards on the north and west sides of the town excavated a lake, communicating with the river, which itself protects it on the east. In addition to this the priests told me that he built there the large and very remarkable temple of Hephaestus.

Next, the priests read to me from a written record the names of three hundred and thirty monarchs, in the same number of generations, all of them Egyptians except eighteen, who were Ethiopians, and one other, who was an Egyptian woman. This last had the same name – Nitocris – as the queen of Babylon. The story was that she ensnared to their deaths hundreds of

Egyptians in revenge for the king her brother, whom his subjects had murdered and forced her to succeed; this she did by constructing an immense underground chamber, in which, under the pretence of opening it by an inaugural ceremony, she invited to a banquet all the Egyptians whom she knew to be chiefly responsible for her brother's death; then, when the banquet was in full swing, she let the river in on them through a large concealed conduit-pipe. The only other thing I was told about her was that after this fearful revenge she flung herself into a room full of ashes, to escape her punishment. The other kings, the priests told me, were in no way distinguished and left nothing to commemorate their reigns, with the exception of the last of them, Moeris, who is remembered by the northern gateway he built for the temple of Hephaestus and the lake with the pyramids in it, which were constructed by his orders. The extent of the lake and the size of the pyramids I will mention later on. As none of the other kings on the priests' roll left any memorial at all, I will pass on to say something of Sesostris, who succeeded them. Sesostris, the priests said, sailed first with a fleet of warships from the Arabian gulf along the coast of the Indian Ocean, subduing the coastal tribes as he went, until he found that shoal water made further progress impossible; then on his return to Egypt (still according to the priests' account) he raised a powerful army and marched across the continent, reducing to subjection every nation in his path. Whenever he encountered a courageous enemy who fought valiantly for freedom, he erected pillars on the spot

inscribed with his own name and country, and a sentence to indicate that by the might of his armed forces
he had won the victory; if, however, a town fell easily
into his hands without a struggle, he made an addition
to the inscription on the pillar – for not only did he
record upon it the same facts as before, but added a
picture of a woman's genitals, meaning to show that
the people of that town were no braver than women.
Thus his victorious progress through Asia continued,
until he entered Europe and defeated the Scythians
and Thracians; this, I think, was the furthest point the
Egyptian army reached for the memorial columns are
to be seen in this part of the country but not beyond.
On his way back Sesostris came to the river Phasis,
and it is quite possible that he here detached a body of
troops from his army and left them behind to settle –
or, on the other hand, it may be that some of his men
were sick of their travels and deserted. I cannot say
with certainty which supposition is the right one. But it
is undoubtedly a fact that the Colchians are of Egyptian
descent. I noticed this myself before I heard anyone
else mention it, and when it occurred to me I asked
some questions both in Colchis and in Egypt, and
found that the Colchians remembered the Egyptians
more distinctly than the Egyptians remembered them.
The Egyptians did, however, say that they thought the
original Colchians were men from Sesostris' army. My
own idea on the subject was based first on the fact that
they have black skins and woolly hair (not that that
amounts to much, as other nations have the same), and
secondly, and more especially, on the fact that the

19

Colchians, the Egyptians, and the Ethiopians are the only races which from ancient times have practised circumcision. The Phoenicians and the Syrians of Palestine themselves admit that they learned the practice from Egypt, and the Syrians who live near the rivers Thermodon and Parthenius, as well as their neighbours the Macronians, say that they learnt it only a short time ago from the Colchians. No other nations use circumcision, and all these are without doubt following the Egyptian lead. As between the Egyptians and the Ethiopians, I cannot say which learned from the other, for the custom is evidently a very ancient one; but I have no doubt that the other nations adopted it as a result of their intercourse with Egypt, and in this belief I am strongly supported by the fact that Phoenicians who have contact with Greece drop the Egyptian usage, and allow their children to go uncircumcised.

And now I think of it, there is a further point of resemblance between the Colchians and Egyptians: they share a method of weaving linen different from that of any other people; and there is also a similarity between them in language and way of living. The linen made in Colchis is known in Greece as Sardonian linen; that which comes from Egypt is called Egyptian.

Most of the memorial pillars which King Sesostris erected in the conquered countries have disappeared, but I have seen some myself in Palestine, with the inscription I mentioned, and the drawing of a woman's genitals. In Ionia also there are two images of Sesostris cut on rock, one on the road from Ephesus to Phocaea, the other on the road between Sardis and Smyrna; in each case the carved figure is nearly seven feet high and represents a man with a spear in his right hand and a bow in his left, and the rest of his equipment to match – partly Egyptian, partly Ethiopian. Across the breast from shoulder to shoulder runs an inscription, cut in the Egyptian sacred script: *By the strength of my shoulders I won this land.* The name and country of the conqueror are not here recorded, and some who have seen the image suppose it to represent Memnon; however, they are wide of the mark, for Sesostris has made the truth plain enough elsewhere.

The priests went on to tell me that Sesostris, on his return home with a host of prisoners from the conquered countries, was met at Daphnae, near Pelusium, by his brother, whom he had left to govern Egypt during his absence, and invited with his sons to a banquet. While they were at dinner, his brother piled faggots round the building and set them on fire. Seeing what had happened, Sesostris at once asked his wife (for she too was a member of the party) what he should do about it, and was advised by her to take two of their sons – of whom there were six – and lay them out over the burning wood to make a bridge by which they might walk through the fire to safety. The king took her advice, with the result that two of his sons were burnt to death, while the others, together with their father, were saved.

Once home again in Egypt, Sesostris punished his brother and proceeded to employ his prisoners of war in various tasks. It was they who were forced to drag the enormous masses of stone which were brought during Sesostris' reign for the temple of Hephaestus, and to dig the dykes which one finds there today, thereby depriving Egypt – though it was far from their intention to do so – of the horses and carriages which were formerly in such common use throughout the country. All Egypt is flat; yet from that time onwards it has been unfit for horses or wheeled traffic because of the innumerable dykes, running in all directions, which cut the country up. The king's object was to supply water to the towns which lay inland at some distance from the river; for previously the people in these towns, when the level of the river fell, had to go short and to drink brackish water from wells. It was this king, moreover, who divided the land into lots and gave everyone a square piece of equal size, from the produce of which he exacted an annual tax. Any man whose holding was damaged by the encroachment of the river would go and declare his loss before the king, who would send inspectors to measure the extent of the loss, in order that he might pay in future a fair proportion of the tax at which his property had been assessed. I think this was the way in which geometry was invented, and passed afterwards into Greece – for knowledge of the sundial and the gnomon and the twelve divisions of the day came into Greece from Babylon.

Sesostris was the only Egyptian king to rule Ethiopia. As memorials of his reign he left stone statues of himself and his wife, each forty-five feet high, and statues thirty feet high of each of his four sons. They were erected in front of the temple of Hephaestus.

Long afterwards the priest of Hephaestus would not allow Darius the king of Persia to erect a statue of himself in front of these, because (as he put it) his deeds had not been as great as the deeds of Sesostris the Egyptian; the conquests of Sesostris, no less extensive than those of Darius, included the Scythians, whom Darius had been unable to subdue; it was not right, therefore, that he should put his statue in front of those dedicated by a monarch whose achievements he had failed to surpass. Darius, they say, admitted the truth of this.

When Sesostris died, he was succeeded by his son Pheros, a prince who undertook no military adventures. He went blind, and the reason for it is explained in the following story; one year the Nile rose to an excessive height, as much as twenty-seven feet, and when all the fields were under water it began to blow hard, so that the river got very rough. The king in insensate rage seized a spear and hurled it into the swirling waters, and immediately thereafter he was attacked by a disease of the eyes, and became blind. He was blind for ten years, and in the eleventh he received an oracle from the city of Buto to the effect that the time of his punishment being now ended, he would recover his sight, if he washed his eyes with the urine of a woman who had never lain with any man except her husband. He tried his wife first, but without success; then he tried other women, a great many, one after another, until at last his sight was restored. Then he collected within the walls of a town, now called Red Clod, all the women except the one whose urine had proved efficacious, set the place on fire, and burnt them to death, town and all; afterwards he married the woman who had been the means of curing him. In gratitude for his recovery he dedicated a number of offerings in all the temples of repute; but the most remarkable of them were two stone obelisks which he set up in the precinct of the temple of the Sun. These are well worth seeing; they are twelve feet broad and a hundred and fifty feet high, each hewn from a single block of stone.

Pheros was succeeded by a native of Memphis, whose name in the Greek language was Proteus. To this day there is a sacred precinct of his at Memphis, very fine and richly adorned, and situated south of the temple of Hephaestus. The whole district hereabouts is known as the Camp of the Tyrians, because the houses in the neighbourhood are occupied by Phoenicians from Tyre. Within the enclosure there is a temple dedicated to the foreign Aphrodite. I should guess, myself, that it was built in honour of Helen the daughter of Tyndareus, not only because I have heard it said that she passed some time at the court of Proteus, but also, and more particularly, because of the description of Aphrodite as 'the foreigner', a title never given to this goddess in any of her other temples. I questioned the priests about the story of Helen, and they told me in reply that Paris was on his way home from Sparta with his stolen bride, when, somewhere in the Aegean sea, he met foul weather, which drove his ship towards Egypt, until at last, the gale continuing as bad as ever, he found himself on the coast, and managed to get ashore at the Salt-pans, in the mouth of the Nile now called the Canopic. Here on the beach there was a temple, which still exists, dedicated to Heracles, and in connexion with it there is a very ancient custom, which has remained unaltered to my day. If a runaway slave takes refuge in this shrine and allows the sacred marks, which are the sign of his submission to the service of the god, to be set upon his body, his master, no matter who he is, cannot lay hands on him. Now some of Paris' servants found out about this and, wishing to get him into trouble, deserted, and fled as suppliants to the temple and told against him the whole story of his abduction of Helen and his wicked treatment of Menelaus. They brought these charges against their master not only before the temple priests, but also before the warden of that mouth of the Nile, a man named Thonis. Thonis at once sent a dispatch to Proteus at Memphis. 'A Trojan stranger (the message ran) has arrived here from Greece, where he has been guilty of an abominable crime: first he seduced the wife of his host, then carried her off together with a great deal of valuable property; and now stress of weather has forced him to land on this coast. Are we to let him sail away again in possession of his stolen goods, or should we confiscate them?' Proteus answered: 'No matter who it is that has committed this crime against his friend, arrest him and send him to me, that I may hear what he can say for himself.' Thonis accordingly arrested Paris, held his ships, and took both him and Helen to Memphis, together with the stolen property and the servants who had taken sanctuary in the temple. On their arrival Proteus asked Paris who he was and where he had come from, and Paris gave him his name and all the details of his family and a true account of his voyage; but when he was further asked how he had got possession of Helen, then, instead of telling the truth, he began to vacillate, until the runaway servants convicted him of lying and told the whole story of his crime. Finally Proteus gave his judgement: 'If,' he said, 'I did not consider it a matter of great importance that I have never yet put to death any stranger who has been forced upon my coasts by stress of weather, I should have punished you for the sake of your Greek host. To be welcomed as a guest, and to repay that kindness by so foul a deed! You are a villain. You seduced your friend's wife, and, as if that were not enough, persuaded her to escape with you on the wings of passion you roused. Even that did not content you – but you must bring with you besides the treasure you have stolen from your host's house. But though I cannot punish a stranger with death, I will not allow you to take away your ill-gotten gains: I will keep this woman and the treasure, until the Greek to whom they belong chooses to come and fetch them. As for you and the companions of your voyage, I give you three days in which to leave my country – and to find an anchorage elsewhere. If you are not gone by then, I shall treat you as enemies.'

This was the account I had from the priests about the arrival of Helen at Proteus' court. I think Homer was familiar with the story; for though he rejected it as less suitable for epic poetry than the one he actually used, he left indications that it was not unknown to him. For instance, when he describes the wanderings of Paris in the *Iliad* (and he has not elsewhere contradicted his account), he says that in the course of them he brought Helen to Sidon in Phoenicia. The passage occurs in the section of the poem where Diomedes performs his great deeds and it runs like this:

> There were the bright robes woven by the women of
>   Sidon,
> Whom the hero Paris, splendid as a god to look on,
> Brought from that city when he sailed the wide sea
> Voyaging with high-born Helen, when he took her
>   home.

There is also a passage in the *Odyssey* alluding to the same fact:

> These drugs of subtle virtue the daughter of Zeus was
>   given
> By an Egyptian woman, Polydamna, wife of Thon;
> For the rich earth of Egypt bears many herbs
> Mixed together, which have power to cure, or to kill.

and, again, Menelaus is made to say to Telemachus:

> In Egypt the gods still stayed me, though I longed to
>   return,
> For I had not paid them their due of sacrifice.

Homer makes it quite clear in these passages that he knew about Paris going out of his way to Egypt – the point of the first I have quoted being that Syria borders on Egypt, and the Phoenicians, to whom Sidon belongs, live in Syria. Another thing which is proved by these passages, and especially by the one about Sidon, is that Homer was not the author of the *Cypria*; for in that poem it is stated that Paris reached Troy with Helen three days after he left Sparta, having had a good voyage with a fair wind and calm sea, whereas we learn from the *Iliad* that he was forced to take her far out of his way – but I must take my leave of Homer and the *Cypria*.

I asked the priests if the Greek story of what happened at Troy had any truth in it, and they gave me in reply some information which they claimed to have had direct from Menelaus himself. This was, that after the abduction of Helen, the Greeks sent a strong force to the Troad in support of Menelaus' cause, and as soon as the men had landed and established themselves on Trojan soil, ambassadors, of whom Menelaus was one, were dispatched to Troy. They were received within the walls of the town, and demanded the restoration of Helen together with the treasure which Paris had stolen, and also satisfaction for the injuries they had received. The Trojans, however, gave them the answer which they always stuck to afterwards – sometimes even swearing to the truth of it: namely, that neither Helen nor the treasure was in their possession, but both were in Egypt, and there was no justice in trying to force them to give satisfaction for property which was being detained by the Egyptian king Proteus. The Greeks, supposing this to be a merely frivolous answer, laid siege to the town, and persisted until it fell; but no Helen was found, and they were still told the same story, until at last they believed it and sent Menelaus to visit Proteus in Egypt. He sailed up the river to Memphis, and when he had given a true account of all that had happened, he was most hospitably entertained and Helen, having suffered no evils, was restored to him with all the rest of his property. Nevertheless, in spite of this generous treatment, Menelaus proved himself no friend to Egypt; for when he wished to leave, but was delayed for a long time by contrary winds, he took two Egytian children and offered them in sacrifice. The discovery of this foul act turned the friendship of the Egyptians to hatred; he was pursued, but managed to escape with his ships to Libya. Where he went afterwards the Egyptians could not say. They told me that they had learned of some of these events by inquiry, but spoke with certain knowledge of those which had taken place in their own country.

This, then, is the version the Egyptian priests gave me of the story of Helen, and I am inclined to accept it for the following reason: had Helen really been in Troy, she would have been handed over to the Greeks with or without Paris' consent; for I cannot believe that either Priam or any other kinsman of his was mad enough to be willing to risk his own and his children's lives and the safety of the city, simply to let Paris continue to live with Helen. If, moreover, that had been their feeling when the troubles began, surely later on, when the Trojans had suffered heavy losses in every battle they fought, and there was never an engagement (if we may believe the epic poems) in which Priam himself did not lose two of his sons, or three, or even more: surely, I repeat, in such circumstances as these, there can be little doubt that, even if Helen had been the wife of Priam the king, he would have given her back to the Greeks, if to do so offered a chance of relief from the suffering which the war had caused. Again, Paris was not heir to the throne, and so could not have been acting as regent for his aged father; for it was Hector, his elder brother and a better man than he, who was to have succeeded on Priam's death, and it was not likely that Hector would put up with his brother's lawless behaviour, especially as it was the cause of much distress both to himself and to every other Trojan besides. The fact is, they did not give Helen up because they had not got her; what they told the Greeks was the truth, and I do not hesitate to declare that the refusal of the Greeks to believe it came of divine volition in order that their utter destruction might plainly prove to mankind that great offences meet with great punishments at the hands of God. This, then, is my own interpretation.

The next king after Proteus was Rhampsinitus, who is remembered by the entrance gates which he erected at the western end of the temple of Hephaestus, and by two statues which face them, each about thirty-eight feet high; the more northerly of the two is called by the Egyptians Summer; the more southerly, Winter. The former they honour and bow down before, but their behaviour towards the latter is quite the reverse.

Rhampsinitus possessed a vast fortune in silver, so

great that no subsequent king came anywhere near it – let alone surpassed it. In order to keep the treasure safe, he proposed to have a stone building put up, with one of its walls forming a part of the outer wall of his palace. The builder he employed had designs upon the treasure and ingeniously contrived to construct the wall in such a way that one of the stone blocks of which it was composed could easily be removed by a couple of men – or even by one. When the new treasury was ready, the king's money was stored away in it; and after the lapse of some years the builder, then on his death-bed, called his two sons and told them how clever he had been, saying that he had planned the device of the moveable stone entirely for their benefit, that they might live in affluence. Then he gave the precise measurements, and instructions for its removal, and told them that if only they kept the secret well, they would be the Royal Treasurers as long as they lived. So the father died and his sons lost no time in setting to work; they came by night to the palace, found the stone in the treasury wall, took it out easily enough and got away with a good haul of silver. The king, on his next visit to the treasury, was surprised to see that some of the vessels in which the money was stored were no longer full, but as the seals were unbroken and all the locks in perfect order, he was at a loss to find the culprit. When the same thing happened again, and yet again, and he found that each time he visited the chamber the level of the money in the jars had still further fallen (for the thieves persisted in their depre-dations), he ordered traps to be made and set near the money-jars. The thieves came as usual, and one of them made his way into the chamber; but, as soon as he approached the money-jar he was after, the trap got him. Realizing his plight, he at once called out to his brother to tell him what had happened, and begged him to come in as quickly as he could and cut off his head, lest the recognition of his dead body should involve both of them in ruin. The brother, seeing the sense of this request, acted upon it without delay; then, having fitted the stone back in its place, went home taking the severed head with him. Next morning the king visited his treasury, and what was his astonishment when he saw in the trap the headless body of the thief, and no sign of damage to the building, or any apparent means of entrance or exit! Much perplexed, he finally decided to have the thief's body hung up outside the wall, and a guard set with orders to arrest and bring before him anyone they might see thereabouts in tears, or showing signs of mourning. Now the young man's mother was deeply distressed by this treatment of her dead son's body, and begged the one who was still alive to do all he possibly could to think of some way of getting it back, and even threatened, if he refused to listen to her, to go to the king and denounce him as the thief. The young man made many excuses, but to no purpose; his mother continued to pester him, until at last he thought of a way out of the difficulty. He filled some skins with wine and loaded them on to donkeys, which he drove to the place where the soldiers were guarding his brother's corpse. Arrived there, he gave a pull on the necks of two or three of the skins, which undid the fastenings. The wine poured out, and he roared and banged his head, as if not knowing which donkey to deal with first, while the soldiers, seeing the wine streaming all over the road, seized their pots and ran to catch it, congratulating themselves on such a piece of luck. The young man swore at them in pretended rage, which the soldiers did their best to soothe, until finally he changed his tune, and, appearing to have recovered his temper, drove the donkeys out of the roadway and began to rearrange the wineskins on their backs. Meanwhile, as he chatted with the soldiers, one of them cracked a joke at his expense and made him laugh, whereupon he made them a present of a wineskin, and without more ado they all sat down to enjoy themselves, and urged their benefactor to join the party and share the drink. The young man let himself be persuaded, and soon, as cup succeeded cup and the soldiers treated him with increasing familiarity, he gave them another skin. Such a quantity of wine was too much for the guards; very drunk and drowsy, they stretched themselves out at full length and fell asleep on the spot. It was now well after dark, and the thief took down his brother's body and as an insult shaved the right cheek of each of the guards. Then he put the corpse on the donkeys' backs and returned home, having done successfully what his mother demanded.

The king was very angry when he learnt that the thief's body had been stolen, and determined at any cost to catch the man who had been clever enough to bring off such a coup. I find it hard to believe the

priests' account of the means he employed to catch him
– but here it is: he sent his own daughter to a brothel
with orders to admit all comers, and to compel each
applicant, before granting him her favours, to tell her
what was the cleverest and wickedest thing that he had
ever done; and if anyone told her the story of the thief,
she was to get hold of him and not allow him to escape.
The girl obeyed her father's orders, and the thief, when
he came to know the reason for what she was doing,
could not resist the temptation to go one better than
the king in ingenuity. He cut the hand and arm from
the body of a man who had just died, and, putting
them under his cloak, went to visit the king's daughter
in her brothel. When she asked him the question which
she had asked all the others, he replied that his wickedest deed was to cut off his brother's head when he was
caught in a trap in the king's treasury, and his cleverest
was to make the soldiers drunk, so that he could take
down his brother's body from the wall where it was
hanging. The girl immediately clutched at him; but
under cover of the darkness the thief pushed towards
her the hand of the corpse, which she seized and held
tight in the belief that it was his own. Then, leaving it
in her grasp, he made his escape through the door.

The cleverness and audacity of this last exploit filled
the king with astonishment and admiration; soon after
the news of it reached him, he went to every town in
Egypt with a promise to the thief, should he give
himself up, not only of a free pardon but of a rich
reward. The thief trusted him and presented himself,
and Rhampsinitus gave him his daughter in marriage,

on the grounds that the thief was the most intelligent of mankind: for the Egyptians surpass everyone else in knowledge, and this man surpassed all the Egyptians.

Another story I heard about Rhampsinitus was, that at a later period he descended alive into what the Greeks call Hades, and there played dice with Demeter, sometimes winning and sometimes losing, and returned to earth with a golden cloth which she had given him as a present. I was told that to mark his descent into the underworld and subsequent return, the Egyptians instituted a festival, which they certainly continued to celebrate in my own day – though I cannot state with confidence that the reason for it is what it was said to be. The priests weave a robe, taking one day only over the process; then they bandage the eyes of one of their number, put the robe into his hands, and lead him to the road which runs to the temple of Demeter. Here they leave him, and it is supposed that he is escorted to the temple, twenty furlongs from the city, by two wolves which afterwards bring him back to where they found him. Anyone may believe these Egyptian tales, if he is sufficiently credulous; as for myself, I keep to the general plan of this book, which is to record the traditions of the various nations just as I heard them related to me.

[. . .]

Snakes with Wings and Gold-digging Ants

Eastward of India lies a desert of sand; indeed of all the inhabitants of Asia of whom we have any reliable information, the Indians are the most easterly – beyond them the country is uninhabitable desert. There are many tribes of Indians, speaking different languages, some pastoral and nomadic, others not. Some live in the marsh-country by the river and eat raw fish, which they catch from boats made of reeds – each boat made from a single joint. The people of this tribe make their clothes from a sort of rush which grows in the river, gathering it and beating it out, and then weaving it into a kind of matting which they wear to cover their chests, like a breastplate. Another tribe further to the east is nomadic, known as the Padaei; they live on raw meat. Among their customs, it is said that when a man falls sick, his closest companions kill him, because, as they put it, their meat would be spoilt if he were allowed to waste away with disease. The invalid, in these circumstances, protests that there is nothing the matter with him – but to no purpose. His friends refuse to accept his protestations, kill him and hold a banquet. Should the sufferer be a woman, her woman friends deal with her in the same way. If anyone is lucky enough to live to an advanced age, he is offered in sacrifice before the banquet – this, however, rarely happens, because most of them will have had some disease or other before they get old, and will consequently have been killed by their friends.

There is another tribe which behaves very differently: they will not take life in any form; they sow no seed, and have no houses and live on a vegetable diet. There is a plant which grows wild in their country, and has seeds in a pod about the size of millet seeds; they gather this, and boil and eat it, pod and all. In this tribe, a sick man will leave his friends and go away to some deserted spot to die – and nobody gives a thought either to his illness or death.

All the Indian tribes I have mentioned copulate in the open like cattle; their skins are all of the same colour, much like the Ethiopians'. Their semen is not white like other peoples', but black like their own skins; the same is to be found in the Ethiopians. Their country is a long way from Persia towards the south, and they were never subject to Darius.

There are other Indians further north, round the city of Caspatyrus and in the country of Pactyica, who in their mode of life resemble the Bactrians. These are the most warlike of the Indian tribes, and it is they who go out to fetch the gold – for in this region there is a sandy desert. There is found in this desert a kind of ant of great size – bigger than a fox, though not so big as a dog. Some specimens, which were caught there, are kept at the palace of the Persian king. These creatures as they burrow underground throw up the sand in heaps, just as ants in Greece throw up the earth, and they are very similar in shape. The sand has a rich content of gold, and this it is that the Indians are after when they make their expeditions into the desert. Each man harnesses three camels abreast, a female, on which he rides, in the middle, and a male on each side in a leading-rein, and takes care that the female is one who has as recently as possible dropped her young. Their camels are as fast as horses, and much more powerful carriers. There is no need for me to describe the camel, for the Greeks are familiar with what it looks like; one thing, however, I will mention, which will be news to them: the camel in its hind legs has four thighs and four knees, and its genitals point backwards towards its tail. That, then, is how these Indians equip themselves for the expedition, and they plan their time-table so as actually to get their hands on the gold during the hottest part of the day, when the heat will have driven the ants underground. In this part of the world the sun is not, as it is elsewhere, hottest at noon, but in the morning: from dawn, that is, until closing-time in the market. During this part of the day the heat is much fiercer than it is at noon in Greece, and the natives are said to soak themselves in water to make it endurable. At midday the heat diminishes and is much the same here as elsewhere, and, as the afternoon goes on, it becomes about equal to what one finds in other countries in the early morning. Towards evening it grows cooler and cooler, until at sunset it is really cold.

When the Indians reach the place where the gold is, they fill the bags they have brought with them with sand, and start for home again as fast as they can go;

for the ants (as is said in the Persians' story) smell them and at once give chase; nothing in the world can touch these ants for speed, so not one of the Indians would get home alive, if they did not make sure of a good start while the ants were mustering their forces. The male camels, who are slower movers than the females, soon begin to drag and are left behind, one after the other, while the females are kept going hard by the memory of their young, who were left at home.

According to the Persians, most of the gold is got in the way I have described; they also mine a certain quantity – but not so much – within their own territory.

It would seem that the remotest parts of the world have the finest products, whereas Greece has far the best and most temperate climate. The most easterly country in the inhabited world is, as I said just now, India; and here both animals and birds are much bigger than elsewhere – if we except the Indian horse, which is inferior in size to the Median breed known as the Nisaean. Gold, too, is found here in immense quantity, either mined, or washed down by rivers, or stolen from the ants in the manner I have described; and there are trees growing wild which produce a kind of wool better than sheep's wool in beauty and quality, which the Indians use for making their clothes. Again, the most southerly country is Arabia; and Arabia is the only place that produces frankincense, myrrh, cassia, cinnamon, and the gum called ledanon. All these, except the myrrh, cause the Arabians a lot of trouble to collect. When they gather frankincense, they burn storax (the gum which is brought into Greece by the Phoenicians) in order to raise a smoke to drive off the flying snakes; these snakes, the same which attempt to invade Egypt, are small in size and of various colours, and great numbers of them keep guard over all the trees which bear the frankincense, and the only way to get rid of them is by smoking them out with storax. The Arabians say that the whole world would swarm with these creatures were it not for a certain peculiar fact – the same thing, incidentally, as keeps down the spread of adders. And indeed it is hard to avoid the belief that divine providence, in the wisdom that one would expect of it, has made prolific every kind of creature which is timid and preyed upon by others, in order to ensure its continuance, while savage and noxious species are comparatively unproductive. Hares, for instance, which are the prey of all sorts of animals, not to mention birds and men, are excessively prolific; they are the only animals in which superfetation occurs, and you will find in a hare's womb young in all stages of development, some with fur on, others with none, others just beginning to form, and others, again, barely conceived. A lioness, on the contrary, the most bold and powerful of beasts, produces but a single cub, once in her life – for she expels from her body not only the cub, but her womb as well – or what is left of it. The reason for this is that when the unborn cub begins to stir, he scratches at the walls of the womb with his claws, which are sharper than any other animal's, and as he grows bigger scrabbles his way further and further through them until, by the time he is about to be born, the womb is almost wholly destroyed. In the same way, if adders and the Arabian flying snakes were able to replace themselves naturally, it would be impossible for men to live. Fortunately, however, they are not; for when they couple, the female seizes the male by the neck at the very moment of the release of the sperm, and hangs on until she has bitten it through. That finishes the male; and the female, too, has to pay for her behaviour, for the young in her belly avenge their father by gnawing at her insides, until they end by eating their way out. Other species of snakes, which are harmless to men, lay eggs and hatch out their young in large numbers. The reason why flying snakes seem so numerous in Arabia is that they are all concentrated in that country – you will not find them anywhere else, whereas adders are common all over the world.

When the Arabians go out to collect cassia, they cover their bodies and faces, all but their eyes, with ox-hides and other skins. The plant grows in a shallow lake which, together with the ground round about it, is infested by winged creatures very like bats, which screech alarmingly and are very pugnacious. They have to be kept from attacking the men's eyes while they are cutting the cassia. The process of collecting cinnamon is still more remarkable. Where it comes from and what country produces it, they do not know; the best some of them can do is to make a fair guess that it grows somewhere in the region where Dionysus was brought up. What they say is that the dry sticks, which we have learnt from the Phoenicians to call cinnamon, are brought by large birds, which carry them to their nests, made of mud, on mountain precipices, which no man can climb, and that the method the Arabians have invented for getting hold of them is to cut up the bodies of dead oxen, or donkeys, or other animals into very large joints, which they carry to the spot in question and leave on the ground near the nests. They then retire to a safe distance and the birds fly down and carry off the joints of meat to their nests, which, not being strong enough to bear the weight, break and fall to the ground. Then the men come along and pick up the cinnamon, which is subsequently exported to other countries. Still more surprising is the way of getting ledanon – or ladanon, as the Arabians call it. Sweet-smelling substance though it is, it is found in a most malodorous place; sticking, namely, like glue in the beards of he-goats who have been browsing amongst the bushes. It is used as an ingredient in many kinds of perfume, and is what the Arabians chiefly burn as incense.

So much for the perfumes: let me only add that the whole country exhales a more than earthly fragrance. One other thing is remarkable enough to deserve a mention – the sheep. There are two kinds, such as are found nowhere else: one kind has such long tails – not less than 4½ feet – that if they were allowed to trail on the ground, they would develop sores from the constant friction; so to obviate this, the shepherds have devised the art of making little carts of wood, and fix one of them under the tail of each sheep. The other kind have flat tails, eighteen inches broad.

The furthest inhabited country towards the south-west is Ethiopia; here gold is found in great abundance, and huge elephants, and ebony, and all sorts of trees growing wild; the men, too, are the tallest in the world, the best-looking, and longest-lived.

[...]

The Dead are Buried in Honey

The following are certain Persian customs which I can describe from personal knowledge. The erection of statues, temples, and altars is not an accepted practice amongst them, and anyone who does such a thing is considered a fool, because, presumably, the Persian religion is not anthropomorphic like the Greek. Zeus, in their system, is the whole circle of the heavens, and they sacrifice to him from the tops of mountains. They also worship the sun, moon, and earth, fire, water, and winds, which are their only original deities: it was later that they learned from the Assyrians and Arabians the cult of Uranian Aphrodite. The Assyrian name for Aphrodite is Mylitta, the Arabian Alilat, the Persian Mitra.

As for ceremonial, when they offer sacrifice to the deities I mentioned, they erect no altar and kindle no fire; the libation, the flute-music, the garlands, the sprinkled meal – all these things they have no use for; but before a ceremony a man sticks a spray of leaves, usually myrtle leaves, into his headdress, takes his victim to some purified place and invokes the deity to whom he wishes to sacrifice. The actual worshipper is not permitted to pray for any personal or private blessing, but only for the king and for the general good of the community, of which he is himself a part. When

44

he has cut up the animal and cooked it, he makes a little heap of the softest green-stuff he can find, preferably clover, and lays all the meat upon it. This done, a Magus (a member of this caste must be always present at sacrifices) utters an incantation over it in a form of words which is supposed to recount the Birth of the Gods. Then after a short interval the worshipper removes the flesh and does what he pleases with it.

Of all days in the year a Persian most distinguishes his birthday, and celebrates it with a dinner of special magnificence. A rich Persian on his birthday will have an ox or a horse or a camel or a donkey baked whole in the oven and served up at table, and the poor some smaller beast. The main dishes at their meals are few, but they have many sorts of dessert, the various courses being served separately. It is this custom that has made them say that the Greeks leave the table hungry, because they never have anything worth mentioning after the first course: they think that if the Greeks did, they should go on eating. They are very fond of wine, and no one is allowed to vomit or urinate in the presence of another person.

If an important decision is to be made, they discuss the question when they are drunk, and the following day the master of the house where the discussion was held submits their decision for reconsideration when they are sober. If they still approve it, it is adopted; if not, it is abandoned. Conversely, any decision they make when they are sober, is reconsidered afterwards when they are drunk.

When Persians meet in the streets one can always

tell by their mode of greeting whether or not they are of the same rank; for they do not speak but kiss – their equals upon the mouth, those somewhat superior on the cheeks. A man of greatly inferior rank prostrates himself in profound reverence. After their own nation they hold their nearest neighbours most in honour, then the nearest but one – and so on, their respect decreasing as the distance grows, and the most remote being the most despised. Themselves they consider in every way superior to everyone else in the world, and allow other nations a share of good qualities decreasing according to distance, the furthest off being in their view the worst. By a similar sort of principle the Medes extended their system of administration and government during the period of their dominance: the various nations governed each other, the Medes being the supreme authority and concerning themselves specially with their nearest neighbours; these in their turn ruling *their* neighbours, who were responsible for the next, and so on.

No race is so ready to adopt foreign ways as the Persian; for instance, they wear the Median costume because they think it handsomer than their own, and their soldiers wear the Egyptian corslet. Pleasures, too, of all sorts they are quick to indulge in when they get to know about them – a notable instance is pederasty, which they learned from the Greeks. Every man has a number of wives, and a much greater number of concubines. After prowess in fighting, the chief proof of manliness is to be the father of a large family of boys. Those who have most sons receive an annual present from the king – on the principle that there is strength in numbers. The period of a boy's education is between the ages of five and twenty, and they are taught three things only: to ride, to use the bow, and to speak the truth. Before the age of five a boy lives with the women and never sees his father, the object being to spare the father distress if the child should die in the early stages of its upbringing. In my view this is a sound practice. I admire also the custom which forbids even the king himself to put a man to death for a single offence, and any Persian under similar circumstances to punish a servant by an irreparable injury. Their way is to balance faults against services, and then, if the faults are greater and more numerous, anger may take its course. They declare that no man has ever yet killed his father or mother; in the cases where this has apparently happened, they are quite certain that inquiry would reveal that the son was either a changeling or born out of wedlock, for they insist that it is most improbable that the actual parent should be killed by his child. What they are forbidden to do, they are forbidden also to mention. They consider telling lies more disgraceful than anything else, and, next to that, owing money. There are many reasons for their horror of debt, but the chief is their conviction that a man who owes money is bound also to tell lies. Sufferers from the scab or from leprosy are isolated and forbidden the city. They say these diseases are punishments for offending the sun, and they expel any stranger who catches them: many Persians drive away even white doves, as if they, too, were guilty of the same

47

offence. They have a profound reverence for rivers: they will never pollute a river with urine or spittle, or even wash their hands in one, or allow anyone else to do so. There is one other peculiarity which one notices about them, though they themselves are unaware of it: all their names, which express magnificence or physical qualities, end in the letter S (the Dorian 'san'). Inquiry will prove this in every case without exception.

All this I am able to state definitely from personal knowledge. There is another practice, however, concerning the burial of the dead, which is not spoken of openly and is something of a mystery: it is that a male Persian is never buried until the body has been torn by a bird or a dog. I know for certain that the Magi have this custom, for they are quite open about it. The Persians in general, however, cover a body with wax and then bury it. The Magi are a peculiar caste, quite different from the Egyptian priests and indeed from any other sort of person. The Egyptian priests make it an article of religion to kill no living creature except for sacrifice, but the Magi not only kill anything, except dogs and men, with their own hands but make a special point of doing so; ants, snakes, crawling animals, birds – no matter what, they kill them indiscriminately. Well, it is an ancient custom, so let them keep it.

[...]

I will give several indications of the wealth and resources of Babylon, but the following is a specially striking one. Apart from normal tribute, the whole

Persian empire is divided into regions for the purpose of furnishing supplies for the king and his army, and for four months out of the twelve the supplies come from Babylonian territory, the whole of the rest of Asia being responsible for the remaining eight. This shows that the resources of Assyria are a third part of the resources of Asia as a whole. It will be seen that the governorship (or satrapy, as the Persians call it) of Assyria is by far the most coveted of all their provincial posts, when one realizes that Tritantaechmes the son of Artabazus, who held it from the king, received an *artaba* of silver every day – the *artaba* is a Persian dry measure of about five bushels, exceeding the Attic *medimnus* by three *choinikes*, or about five pints. He also had as his personal property, in addition to war horses, eight hundred stallions and sixteen thousand mares, twenty for each stallion, and so many Indian dogs that four large villages in the plain were exempted from other charges on condition of supplying them with food. This will give an idea of the wealth of the governor of Babylon.

The rainfall of Assyria is slight and provides enough moisture only to burst the seed and start the root growing, but to swell the grain and bring it to maturity artificial irrigation is used, not, as in Egypt, by the natural flooding of the river, but by hand-worked swipes. Like Egypt, the whole country is intersected by dykes; the largest of them has to be crossed in boats and runs in a south-easterly direction from the Euphrates until it joins another river, the Tigris, on which Nineveh was built. As a grain-bearing country

49

Assyria is the richest in the world. No attempt is made there to grow figs, grapes, or olives or any other fruit trees, but so great is the fertility of the grain fields that they normally produce crops of two-hundredfold, and in an exceptional year as much as three-hundredfold. The blades of wheat and barley are at least three inches wide. As for millet and sesame, I will not say to what an astonishing size they grow, though I know well enough; but I also know that people who have not been to Babylonia have refused to believe even what I have said already about its fertility. The only oil these people use is made from sesame; date-palms grow everywhere, mostly of the fruit-bearing kind, and the fruit supplies them with food, wine, and honey. The method of cultivation is the same as for figs, particularly in regard to the practice of taking the fruit of what the Greeks call the 'male' palm and tying it into the 'female' or date-bearing tree, to allow the gall-fly to enter the fruit and ripen it and prevent it from dropping off. For it is a fact that the male palms have the gall-fly in their fruit, like wild figs.

I will next describe the thing which surprised me most of all in this country, after Babylon itself: I mean the boats which ply down the Euphrates to the city. These boats are circular in shape and made of hide; they build them in Armenia to the northward of Assyria, where they cut ribs of osiers to make the frames and then stretch watertight skins taut on the underside for the body of the craft; they are not fined-off or tapered in any way at bow or stern, but quite round like a shield. The men fill them with straw, put the cargo on board – mostly wine in palm-wood casks – and let the current take them downstream. They are controlled by two men; each has a paddle which he works standing up, one in front drawing his paddle towards him, the other behind giving it a backward thrust. The boats vary a great deal in size; some are very big, the biggest of all having a capacity of some hundred and thirty tons. Every boat carries a live donkey – the larger ones several – and when they reach Babylon and the cargoes have been offered for sale, the boats are broken up, the frames and straw sold and the hides loaded on the donkeys' backs for the return journey overland to Armenia. It is quite impossible to paddle the boats upstream because of the strength of the current, and that is why they are constructed of hide instead of wood. Back in Armenia with their donkeys, the men build another lot of boats to the same design.

The dress of the Babylonians consists of a linen tunic reaching to the feet with a woollen one over it, and a short white cloak on top; they have their own fashion in shoes, which resemble the slippers one sees in Boeotia. They grow their hair long, wear turbans, and perfume themselves all over; everyone owns a seal and a walking-stick specially made for him, with a device carved on the top of it, an apple or rose or lily or eagle or something of the sort; for it is not the custom to have a stick without some such ornament. I will say no more about dress and so forth, but will go on to describe some of their practices. The most ingenious in my opinion is a custom which, I understand, they share with the Eneti in

Illyria. In every village once a year all the girls of marriageable age used to be collected together in one place, while the men stood round them in a circle; an auctioneer then called each one in turn to stand up and offered her for sale, beginning with the best-looking and going on to the second best as soon as the first had been sold for a good price. Marriage was the object of the transaction. The rich men who wanted wives bid against each other for the prettiest girls, while the humbler folk, who had no use for good looks in a wife, were actually paid to take the ugly ones, for when the auctioneer had got through all the pretty girls he would call upon the plainest, or even perhaps a crippled one, to stand up, and then ask who was willing to take the least money to marry her – and she was offered to whoever accepted the smallest sum. The money came from the sale of the beauties, who in this way provided dowries for their ugly or misshapen sisters. It was illegal for a man to marry his daughter to anyone he happened to fancy, and no one could take home a girl he had bought without first finding a backer to guarantee his intention of marrying her. In cases of disagreement between husband and wife the law allowed the return of the purchase money. Anyone who wished could come even from a different village to buy a wife.

This admirable practice has now fallen into disuse and they have of late years hit upon another scheme, namely the prostitution of all girls of the lower classes to provide some relief from the poverty which followed upon the conquest with its attendant hardship and general ruin.

Next in ingenuity to the old marriage custom is their treatment of disease. They have no doctors, but bring their invalids out into the street, where anyone who comes along offers the sufferer advice on his complaint, either from personal experience or observation of a similar complaint in others. Anyone will stop by the sick man's side and suggest remedies which he has himself proved successful in whatever the trouble may be, or which he has known to succeed with other people. Nobody is allowed to pass a sick person in silence; but everyone must ask him what is the matter. They bury their dead in honey, and their dirges for the dead are like the Egyptian ones. When a Babylonian has had intercourse with his wife, he sits over incense to fumigate himself, with his wife opposite doing the same, and at daybreak they both wash. Before they have washed they will not touch any household utensils. In this they resemble the Arabians.

There is one custom amongst these people which is wholly shameful: every woman who is a native of the country must once in her life go and sit in the temple of Aphrodite and there give herself to a strange man. Many of the rich women, who are too proud to mix with the rest, drive to the temple in covered carriages with a whole host of servants following behind, and there wait; most, however, sit in the precinct of the temple with a band of plaited string round their heads – and a great crowd they are, what with some sitting there, others arriving, others going away – and through them all gangways are marked off running in every direction for the men to pass along and make their choice. Once a woman has taken her seat she is not allowed to go home until a man has thrown a silver coin into her lap and taken her outside to lie with her. As he throws the coin, the man has to say, 'In the name of the goddess Mylitta' – that being the Assyrian name for Aphrodite. The value of the coin is of no consequence; once thrown it becomes sacred, and the law forbids that it should ever be refused. The woman has no privilege of choice – she must go with the first man who throws her the money. When she has lain with him, her duty to the goddess is discharged and she may go home, after which it will be impossible to seduce her by any offer, however large. Tall, handsome women soon manage to get home again, but the ugly ones stay a long time before they can fulfil the condition which the law demands, some of them, indeed, as much as three or four years. There is a custom similar to this in parts of Cyprus.

In addition to the general practices I have mentioned, there is one which is peculiar to three of their clans: these people live entirely on fish which they catch and dry in the sun and then pound in a mortar: the smooth powder is then strained through muslin and eaten either kneaded into cakes or baked like a sort of bread, according to taste.

[. . .]

In their dress and way of living the Massagetae are like the Scythians. Some ride, some do not – for they use both infantry and cavalry. They have archers and spearmen and are accustomed to carry the 'sagaris', or battle-axe. The only metals they use are gold and bronze: bronze for spearheads, arrow-points, and battle-axe, and gold for headgear, belts, and girdles. Similarly they give their horses bronze breastplates, and use gold about the bridle, bit, and cheek-pieces. Silver and iron are unknown to them, none being found in the country, though it produces bronze and gold in unlimited quantity. As to their customs: every man has a wife, but all wives are used promiscuously. The Greeks believe this to be a Scythian custom; but it is not – it belongs to the Massagetae. If a man wants a woman, all he does is to hang up his quiver in front of her waggon and then enjoy her without misgiving. They have one way only of determining the appropriate time to die, namely this: when a man is very old, all his relatives give a party and include him in a general sacrifice of cattle; then they boil the flesh and eat it. This they consider to be the best sort of death. Those who die of disease are not eaten but buried, and it is held a misfortune not to have lived long enough to be sacrificed. They have no agriculture, but live on meat and fish, of which there is an abundant supply in the Araxes. They are milk-drinkers. The only god they worship is the sun, to which they sacrifice horses: the idea behind this is to offer the swiftest of mortal creatures to the swiftest of the gods.

[. . .]

The Pillar of the Sky

The following is a description of the Libyan tribes
in their order: starting from Egypt, the first are the
Adyrmachidae, whose way of living is more or less
Egyptian in character. They dress like the rest of the
Libyans. Their women wear a bronze ring on each leg,
and grow their hair long; when they catch a bug on
their persons, they give it bite for bite before throwing
it away. They are the only Libyan tribe to follow this
practice, as also that of taking girls who are about to
be married to see the king. Any girl who catches his
fancy, leaves him a maid no longer. This tribe extends
from the Egyptian border as far as the port called
Plynus.

Next come the Giligamae, whose territory runs westward as far as the island of Aphrodisias. In between lies
Platea, the island off the coast where the Cyrenaeans
first settled, and on the mainland is the Harbour of
Menelaus, and Aziris where the Cyrenaeans also lived
for a time. It is in this part of the country that silphium
begins to be found, and extends all the way from Platea
to the mouth of the Syrtis. The Giligamae live in much
the same sort of way as the other tribes. Next to the
westward are the Asbystae; their territory lies further
inland than Cyrene, and does not extend to the coast,
which is occupied by the Cyrenaeans. This tribe is con-

spicuous amongst the Libyans for its use of four-horse chariots, and in its general way of life does its best to imitate that of Cyrene. Westward, again, are the Auschisae, who live south of Barca and touch the sea near Euesperides. Within their territory is the small tribe of the Bacales, who reach the coast near Tauchira, a town belonging to Barca; they live in the same sort of way as the people south of Cyrene. Still proceeding in a westerly direction, one comes next to the Nasamones, a numerous tribe, who in the summer leave their cattle on the coast and go up country to a place called Augila for the date harvest. The date-palms here grow in large numbers and to a great size, and are all of the fruit-bearing kind. These people also catch locusts, which they dry in the sun and grind up fine; then they sprinkle the powder on milk and drink it. Each of them has a number of wives, which they use in common, like the Massagetae – when a man wants to lie with a woman, he puts up a pole to indicate his intention. It is the custom, at a man's first marriage, to give a party, at which the bride is enjoyed by each of the guests in turn; they take her one after another, and then give her a present – something or other they have brought with them from home. In the matter of oaths, their practice is to swear by those of their countrymen who had the best reputation for integrity and valour, laying their hands upon their tombs; and for purposes of divination they go to sleep, after praying, on the graves of their forebears, and take as significant any dream they may have. When two men make a solemn compact, each drinks from the other's hand, and if there is no liquid available, they take some dust from the ground and lick it up.

The neighbours of the Nasamones are the Psylli – but they no longer exist. There is a story which I repeat as the Libyans tell it: that the south wind dried up the water in their storage tanks, so that they were left with none whatever, as their territory lies wholly within the Syrtis. Upon this they held a council, and having unanimously decided to declare war on the south wind, they marched out to the desert, where the wind blew and buried them in sand. The whole tribe was wiped out, and the Nasamones occupied their former domain.

Further inland to the southward, in the part of Libya where wild beasts are found, live the Garamantes, who avoid all intercourse with men, possess no weapons of war, and do not know how to defend themselves. Along the coast to the westward the neighbours of the Nasamones are the Macae. These people wear their hair in the form of a crest, shaving it close on either side of the head and letting it grow long in the middle; in war they carry ostrich skins for shields. The river Cinyps, which rises on a hill called the Hill of the Graces, runs through their territory to the sea. The Hill of the Graces is about twenty-five miles inland, and is densely wooded, unlike the rest of Libya so far described, which is bare of trees.

Next come the Gindanes. The women of this tribe wear leather bands round their ankles, which are supposed to indicate the number of their lovers: each woman puts on one band for every man she has gone to bed with, so that whoever has the greatest number enjoys the greatest reputation because she has been loved by the greatest number of men. Within the territory of the Gindanes a headland runs into the sea, and it is here that the Lotophagi live, a tribe which lives exclusively on the fruit of the lotus. The lotus fruit is about as big as a mastic-berry, and as sweet as a date. The Lotophagi also make wine from it.

Next along the coast are the Machlyes, who also make use of the lotus, but to a lesser extent than the Lotophagi. Their territory reaches to a large river called Triton, which flows into the great lagoon of Tritonis. In the lagoon there is an island named Phla, and there is said to be an oracle to the effect that the Lacedaemonians should send settlers there. The story is also told of how Jason, when he had finished building the *Argo* under Mt Pelion, put on board, in addition to the usual offerings, a bronze tripod, and set sail to round the Peloponnese on his way to Delphi. Off Cape Malea he was caught by a northerly blow and carried to Libya, where, before he could get his bearings, he found himself in the shoal water off the lagoon of Tritonis. How to get clear was a problem; but at that moment Triton appeared and told Jason to give him the tripod, in return for which he would show him the channel and let them all get away in safety. Jason did as he was asked, whereupon Triton showed him the course to steer in order to clear the shallows. He then placed the tripod in his own temple, after uttering over it in full detail, for the benefit of Jason's crew, the prophecy that when a descendant of the *Argo*'s company should carry off the tripod, it was unavoidably decreed by fate that a hundred Grecian cities should then be built on the shores of Lake Tritonis. The Libyans in the neighbourhood got to know of this prophecy, and hid the tripod.

The people next to the Machlyes are the Auses; both these tribes live on the shores of the lagoon, and the river Triton forms the boundary between them. The Machlyes let the hair grow on the back of their heads, the Auses on the front. They hold an annual festival in honour of Athene, at which the girls divide themselves into two groups and fight each other with stones and sticks; they say this rite had come down to them from time immemorial, and by its performance they pay honour to their native deity – which is the same as our Greek Athene. If any girl, during the course of the battle, is fatally injured and dies, they say it is a proof that she is no maiden. Before setting them to fight, they pick out the best-looking girl and dress her up publicly in a full suit of Greek armour and a Corinthian helmet; then they put her in a chariot and drive her round the lagoon. How they dressed these girls before there were Greeks settled in the neighbourhood, I cannot say; presumably the armour they used was Egyptian – for I am prepared to maintain that both shields and helmets were introduced into Greece from Egypt. There is a belief amongst these people that Athene is the daughter of Poseidon and the Triton lake, but that having some quarrel with her father she put herself at the disposal of Zeus, who made her his own daughter. The women of the tribe are common property; there are no married couples living together, and intercourse is casual, like that of animals. When a child is fully grown, the men hold a meeting every third month, and it is considered to belong to the one it most closely resembles.

I have now mentioned all the pastoral tribes along the Libyan coast. Up country further to the south lies the region where wild beasts are found, and beyond that there is a great belt of sand, stretching from Thebes in Egypt to the Pillars of Heracles. Along this belt, separated from one another by about ten days' journey, are little hills formed of lumps of salt, and from the top of each gushes a spring of cold, sweet water. Men live in the neighbourhood of these springs – beyond the wild beasts' region, they are the furthest south, towards the desert, of any human beings. The first of them, ten days' journey from Thebes, are the Ammonians, with their temple derived from that of the Theban Zeus – I have already pointed out how the image of Zeus in both temples has a ram's face. They have another spring there, of which the water is tepid in the early morning and cools down towards market time; by noon it is very cold, and that is the moment when they water their gardens; then, as the days draw towards evening, the chill gradually goes off it, until by sunset it is tepid again; after that it gets hotter and hotter as the night advances, and at midnight it boils furiously. Then, after midnight, the process is reversed, and it steadily cools off until dawn. The spring is known as the Fountain of the Sun.

Ten days' journey west of the Ammonians, along the belt of sand, there is another similar salt-hill and spring. This place, called Augila, is also inhabited, and it is here that the Nasamonians come for their date harvest. Again at the same distance to the west is a salt-hill and spring, just as before, with date-palms of the fruit-bearing kind, as in the other springs; and here live the Garamantes, a very numerous tribe of people, who spread soil over the salt to sow their seed in. From these people is the shortest route – thirty days' journey – to the Lotophagi; and it is amongst them that the cattle are found which walk backwards as they graze. The reason for this curious habit is provided by the formation of their horns, which bend forwards and downwards; this prevents them from moving forwards in the ordinary way, for, if they tried to do so, their horns would stick in the ground. In other respects they are just like ordinary cattle – except for the thickness and toughness of their hide. The Garamantes hunt the Ethiopian troglodytes, in four-horse chariots, for these troglodytes are exceedingly swift of foot – more so than any people of whom we have any information. They eat snakes and lizards and other reptiles and speak a language like no other, but squeak like bats.

Ten days' journey from the Garamantes is yet another hill and spring – this time the home of the Atarantes, the only people in the world, so far as our knowledge goes, to do without names. Atarantes is the collective name – but individually they have none. They curse the sun as it rises and call it by all sorts of opprobrious names, because it wastes and burns both themselves and their land. Once more at a distance of ten days' journey there is a salt-hill, a spring, and a tract of inhabited country, and adjoining it rises Mt

Atlas. In shape the mountain is a slender cone, and it is so high that according to report the top cannot be seen, because summer and winter it is never free of cloud. The natives (who are known as the Atlantes, after the mountains) call it the Pillar of the Sky. They are said to eat no living creature, and never to dream.

Thus far I am able to give the names of the tribes who inhabit the sand-belt, but beyond this point my knowledge fails. I can affirm, however, that the belt continues to the Pillars of Heracles and beyond, and that at regular intervals of ten days' journey are salt-hills and springs, with people living in the neighbourhood. The houses are all built of salt-blocks – an indication that there is no rain in this part of Libya; for if there were, salt walls would collapse. The salt which is mined there is of two colours, white and purple. South of the sand-belt, in the interior, lies a waterless desert, without rain or trees or animal life, or a drop of moisture of any kind.

The coast of Libya, then, between Egypt and Lake Tritonis is occupied by nomads living on meat and milk – though they do not breed pigs, and abstain from cows' meat for the same reason as the Egyptians. Even at Cyrene women think it is wrong to eat heifers' meat, out of respect for the Egyptian Isis, in whose honour they celebrate both fasts and festivals. At Barca the women avoid eating pigs' flesh, as well as cows'. West of Tritonis, nomad tribes are no longer found; the people are quite different, not only in their general way of life, but in the treatment of their children. Many of the nomads – perhaps all, but I cannot be certain about this – when their children are four years old, burn the veins on their heads, and sometimes on their temples, with a bit of greasy wool, as a permanent cure for catarrh. For this reason they are said to be the healthiest people in the world – indeed, it is true enough that they are healthier than any other race we know of, though I cannot be too certain that this is the reason. Anyway, about the fact of their health there is no doubt. Should the cauterizing of the veins bring on convulsions, they have discovered that the effective remedy is to sprinkle goat's urine on the child – I repeat in all this what is said by the Libyans. When the nomad tribes sacrifice, the process is to begin by cutting off the victim's ear, which they throw over the house as a preliminary offering, and then to wring the animal's neck. They sacrifice to the sun and moon, the worship of which is common to all the Libyans, though those who live round Lake Tritonis sacrifice chiefly to Athene, and, after her, to Triton and Poseidon. It is evident, I think, that the Greeks took the clothing and 'aegis' with which they adorn statues of Athene from the dress of the Libyan women; for except that the latter is of leather and has fringes of leather thongs instead of snakes, there is no other point of difference. Moreover, the word 'aegis' itself shows that the dress represented in statues of Athene is derived from Libya; for Libyan women wear goatskins with the hair stripped off, dyed red and fringed at the edges, and it was from these skins that the Greeks took their word 'aegis'. I think too that the crying of women at religious ceremonies also originated in Libya – for the Libyan women are much addicted to this practice, and they do it very beautifully. Another thing the Greeks learnt from Libya was to harness four horses to a chariot. The nomad Libyans – except the Nasamonians – bury their dead just as in Greece; the Nasamonians, however, bury them in a sitting position, and take care when anyone is dying to make him sit up, and not to let him die flat on his back. Their houses, which are portable, are made of the dry haulms of some plant, knit together with rush ropes.

West of the Triton, and beyond the Auses, Libya is inhabited by tribes who live in ordinary houses and practise agriculture. First come the Maxyes, a people who grow their hair on the right side of their heads and shave it off on the left. They stain their bodies red and claim to be descended from the men of Troy. The country round here, and the rest of Libya to the westward, has more forest and a greater number of wild animals than the region which the nomads occupy. The latter – that is, eastern Libya – is low-lying and sandy as far as the river Triton, whereas the agricultural region to the west is very hilly, and abounds with forest and animal life. It is here that the huge snakes are found – and lions, elephants, bears, asps, and horned asses, not to mention dog-headed men, headless men with eyes in their breasts (I merely repeat what the Libyans say), wild men and wild women, and a great many other creatures by no means of a fabulous kind. In the nomads' country none of these occur; instead, one finds white-rump antelopes, gazelles, deer, asses – not the horned sort but a different species which can do without water; it is a fact that they do not drink – another kind of antelope, about as big as an ox, the horns of which are used for making the curved sides of lyres, foxes, hyaenas, hedgehogs, wild rams, jackals, panthers, and others, including land-crocodiles like huge lizards, four and a half feet long, ostriches, and small snakes with a single horn. All these are found, together with other animals common elsewhere, with the exception of the stag and the wild boar, of which there are none at all in Libya. There are, however, three kinds of mice, called respectively *dipodes*, *zegeries*, and *echines* – also weasels which are found amongst the silphium, and resemble those at Tartessus. So much, then, for the animal life in that part of Libya where the nomads are: I have made it as full and accurate as my extensive inquiries permit.

Continuing westward from the Maxyes, one comes next to the Zaueces: amongst this people the drivers of the war-chariots are the women. Their neighbours are the Gyzantes, whose country is very well supplied with honey – much of it made by bees, but even more by confectioners. Everybody here paints himself red and eats monkeys, of which there is an abundant supply in the hills. Off the coast, according to the Carthaginian account, is an island called Cyrauis, about twenty-five miles long, but narrow, which can be reached on foot from the main land and is full of olive-trees and vines. In the island is a lake, and the native girls dip feathers smeared with pitch into the mud at the bottom of it, and bring up gold dust – again, I merely record the current story, without guaranteeing the truth of it. It may, however, be true enough; for I have myself seen something similar in Zacynthus, where pitch is fetched up from the water in a lake. There are a number of lakes – or ponds – in Zacynthus, of which the largest measures seventy feet each way and has a depth of two fathoms. The process is to tie a branch of myrtle on to the end of a pole, which is then thrust down to the bottom of this pond; the pitch sticks to the myrtle, and is thus brought to the surface. It smells like bitumen, but in all other respects it is better than the pitch of Pieria. It is then poured into a trench near the pond, and when a good quantity has been collected, it is removed from the trench and transferred to jars. Anything that falls into this pond, passes underground and comes up again in the sea, a good half mile distant. In view of all this, the account of what happens in the island off Libya may quite possibly be true.

The Carthaginians also say that they trade with a race of men who live in a part of Libya beyond the Pillars of Heracles. On reaching this country, they unload their goods, arrange them tidily along the beach, and then, returning to their boats, raise a smoke. Seeing the smoke, the natives come down to the beach, place on the ground a certain quantity of gold in exchange for the goods, and go off again to a distance. The Carthaginians then come ashore and take a look at the gold; and if they think it represents a fair price for their wares, they collect it and go away; if, on the other hand, it seems too little, they go back aboard and wait, and the natives come and add to the gold until they are satisfied. There is perfect honesty on both sides; the Carthaginians never touch the gold until it equals in value what they have offered for sale, and the natives never touch the goods until the gold has been taken away.

I have now mentioned all the Libyans whose names I am acquainted with; most of them cared nothing for the king of Persia, either then or now. One other thing I can add about this country: so far as one knows, it is inhabited by four races, and four only, of which two are indigenous and two not. The indigenous peoples are the Libyans and Ethiopians, the former occupying the northerly, the latter the more southerly, parts; the immigrants are the Phoenicians and Greeks. I do not think the country can be compared for the fertility of its soil with either Asia or Europe, with the single exception of the region called Cinyps – so named after the river which waters it. This region, however, is quite different from the rest of Libya, and is as good for cereal crops as any land in the world. The soil here, unlike the soil elsewhere, is black and irrigated by springs; it has no fear of drought on the one hand, or of damage, on the other, from excessive rain (it does, by the way, rain in that part of Libya). The yield of the harvests is equal to the yield in Babylonia. There is also good soil at Euesperides – in the best years it will yield a hundred-fold – but the yield in Cinyps is three times as great. The land of Cyrene, the highest of that part of Libya which is inhabited by nomads, has the remarkable peculiarity of three separate harvest-seasons: first, the crops near the coast ripen and are ready for cutting or picking; then, when these are in, the crops in what they call the hill-country – the middle region above the coastal belt – are ready for harvesting; and lastly, when this second harvest is over, the crops in the highest tract of country are ripe and ready, so that by the time the first harvest is all eaten or drunk, the last comes in – making, for the fortunate people of Cyrene, a continuous harvest of eight months on end. So much for this subject.

[. . .]

Fish-eaters and the Crystal Coffin

It was against Amasis[1] that Cyrus' son Cambyses[2] marched at the head of an army drawn from various subject nations and including both Ionian and Aeolian Greeks. His pretext was as follows. Cyrus had sent to Amasis to ask for the services of the best oculist in Egypt, and the one who was selected, in resentment at being torn from his wife and family and handed over to the Persians, suggested to Cambyses by way of revenge that he should ask for Amasis' daughter in marriage, knowing that consent would cause the Egyptian king personal distress, and that refusal would embroil him with Cambyses. Cambyses did as the man suggested, and sent a representative to Egypt to make the request. Amasis, who dreaded the power of Persia, and was well aware that Cambyses wanted his daughter not as a wife but as a concubine, found himself in an awkward position, and unable to say either yes or no. Now there was a daughter of the late King Apries, a tall and beautiful girl named Nitetis, the last survivor of her family, and Amasis, after thinking the matter over, decided to dress her up like a princess in fine clothes adorned with gold, and send her to Persia as his own daughter. This he did; and some time later,

---

[1] king of Egypt   [2] king of Persia

when Cambyses happened to address her by her father's name, she replied: 'My lord, you do not know how Amasis has cheated you; he dressed me in gorgeous clothes and sent me to you as his own daughter – but indeed I am not; I am the daughter of Apries, his master, whom he killed when he led the Egyptians to rebel against him.' It was these words, and the cause of quarrel they disclosed, which, according to the Persian account, brought down upon Egypt the wrath of Cambyses, son of Cyrus. The Egyptians, on the other hand, claim that Cambyses was the son of Nitetis, Apries' daughter, and was thus a native of their own country – for it was Cyrus, they say, not Cambyses, who sent to Amasis to demand his daughter. The claim, however, is not justified by facts; for knowing as they do – none better – the laws of Persia, they could not fail to be aware, first, that Persian usage bars a bastard from the succession so long as there is a legitimate heir, and, secondly, that Cambyses was the son of Cassandane, daughter of Pharnaspes, one of the Achaemenidae, and not of this Egyptian woman. The fact is, they wish to claim kinship with Cyrus, and pervert the truth to justify their claim. There is also another story current, but not, I think, a convincing one: namely, that a Persian woman paid a visit to Cyrus' wives, and greatly admired the fine tall sons which she saw standing by Cassandane's side. Hearing her praises, Cassandane, who was vexed with Nitetis, said: 'In spite of my beautiful children Cyrus treats me with contempt and gives all his attention to that woman he got from Egypt.' 'Well then, mother,' exclaimed Cambyses, the elder of her two sons, 'when I'm a man, I'll turn Egypt upside-down for you.' He was only about ten when he astonished the women by making this promise, but he never forgot it; for when he grew up and had ascended the throne, he did, indeed, invade Egypt.

There was another thing, quite different from all this, which helped to bring about the Egyptian expedition. One of the Greek mercenaries of Amasis, a Halicarnassian called Phanes, a brave and intelligent soldier, being dissatisfied for some reason or other with Amasis, escaped from Egypt by sea, with the object of getting an interview with Cambyses. As he was a person of consequence in the army and had very precise knowledge of the internal condition of Egypt, Amasis was anxious to catch him and sent the most trustworthy of his eunuchs to pursue him in a trireme. He was caught in Lycia but not brought back; for getting his guards to drink themselves stupid, he outwitted his captor and made good his escape to Persia. Cambyses was anxious to launch his attack on Egypt and was wondering how best he could cross the desert, when Phanes arrived, and not only revealed to him all the secrets of Amasis, but also advised him that the best way of getting his army through the desert would be to send to the Arabian king and ask for a safe-conduct.

The only entrance into Egypt is through this desert. From Phoenicia to the boundaries of Gaza the country belongs to the Syrians known as 'Palestinian': from Gaza, a town, I should say, not much smaller than Sardis, the trading ports as far as Ienysus belong to the king of Arabia; from there as far as Lake Serbonis, near which Mt Casius runs down to the sea, it is once more Syrian territory; and after Lake Serbonis (where Typhon is supposed to be hidden) Egypt begins. The whole area between Ienysus on the one side, and Mt Casius and the Lake on the other – and it is of consider-able extent, not less than three days' journey – is desert and completely without water.

I will now mention something of which few voyagers to Egypt are aware. Throughout the year, not only from all parts of Greece but from Phoenicia as well, wine is imported into Egypt in earthenware jars; yet one might say that not a single empty wine-jar is to be seen anywhere in the country. The obvious question is: what becomes of them? I will explain. The local official of each place has orders to collect all the jars from his town and send them to Memphis, and the people of Memphis have to fill them with water and send them to this tract of desert in Syria. In this way every fresh jar of wine imported into Egypt, and there emptied of its contents, finds its way into Syria to join the previous ones. It was the Persians, immediately after their conquest of Egypt, who devised this means of storing water in the desert, and so making the pass-age into the country practicable; but at the time of which I am speaking there was no water at all, so Cambyses took the advice of his Halicarnassian friend Phanes, and sent to the Arabian king with a request for safe-conduct. The request was granted, and pledges were exchanged between the two parties.

No nation regards the sanctity of a pledge more seriously than the Arabs. When two men wish to make

a solemn compact, they get the service of a third, who
stands between them and with a sharp stone cuts the
palms of their hands near the base of the thumb; then
he takes a little tuft of wool from their clothes, dips it
in the blood and smears the blood on seven stones
which lie between them, invoking as he does so, the
names of Dionysus and Urania; then the person who
is giving the pledge, commends the stranger – or fellow
citizen, as the case may be – to his friends, who in their
turn consider themselves equally bound to honour it.
The only gods the Arabs recognize are Dionysus and
Urania; the way they cut their hair – all round in a
circle, with the temples shaved – is, they say, in imita-
tion of Dionysus. Dionysus in their language is Orotalt,
and Urania Alilat.

When the Arabian king had made his vow of friendship with the messengers of Cambyses, the method
he devised of helping the Egyptian army was to fill
camel-skins with water, load them on to all his live
camels, and so convey them to the desert, where he
awaited the arrival of the troops. That, at any rate, is
the more credible account of his procedure; there is
also another, which I ought to mention since it too
is told, though it is not so easy to believe. According to
this, the Arabian king had cow-hides and other skins
stitched together to form a pipe long enough to reach
from the Corys – a large river in Arabia which runs
into the Red Sea – all the way to the desert; here he
had large reservoirs constructed, filled them by means
of the pipe, and so stored the water. The water was
brought to three separate places, over a total distance

– between river and desert – of a twelve days' journey.

Psammenitus, Amasis' son, took up a position on the Pelusian mouth of the Nile, to await the attack of Cambyses. Amasis had died before the invasion actually began, after a reign of forty-four years, during which he had suffered no serious disaster. His body was embalmed and buried in the sepulchre he had himself built in the temple of Athene in Sais. In the reign of his successor Psammenitus, an unparalleled event occurred – rain fell at Thebes, a thing which the men of that city say had never happened before, or has ever happened since till my day. Normally, in upper Egypt no rain falls at all; but on this occasion it did – a light shower.

The Persians crossed the desert, took up a position near the Egyptian army, and prepared for an engagement. Before the battle the Greek and Carian mercenaries who were serving with the Egyptians contrived the following against Phanes in their anger at his bringing a foreign army against Egypt: they seized his sons, whom he had left behind, and brought them to the camp, where they made sure their father could see them; then, placing a bowl in the open ground between the two armies, they led the boys up to it one by one, and cut their throats over it. Not one was spared, and when the last was dead, they poured wine and water on to the blood in the bowl, and every man in the mercenary force drank. That done, the fight began; and after a hard struggle and heavy casualties on both sides, the Egyptians were routed.

At the place where this battle was fought I saw a

great marvel which the natives had told me about. The bones still lay there, those of the Persian dead separate from those of the Egyptian, just as they were originally divided, and I noticed that the skulls of the Persians are so thin that the merest touch with a pebble will pierce them, but those of the Egyptians, on the other hand, are so tough that it is hardly possible to break them with a blow from a stone. I was told, very credibly, that the reason was that the Egyptians shave their heads from childhood, so that the bone of the skull is hardened by the action of the sun – this is also why they hardly ever go bald, baldness being rarer in Egypt than anywhere else. This, then, explains the thickness of their skulls; and the thinness of the Persians' skulls rests upon a similar principle: namely that they have always worn felt skull-caps, to guard their heads from the sun. I also observed the same thing at Papremis, where the Persians serving under Achaemenes, the son of Darius, were destroyed by Inarus the Libyan.

After their defeat, the Egyptians fled in disorder and shut themselves up in Memphis. Cambyses called upon them to come to terms, sending a Persian herald up the river to the town in a Mytilenean vessel; but directly they saw the ship coming into the town, they rushed out from the walls in a body, smashed up the ship, tore everyone on board limb from limb, and carried the bits back inside the walls. They then stood a siege, but after a time surrendered. The neighbouring Libyans were alarmed by the fate of Egypt and gave themselves up without a battle, agreeing to pay tribute and sending presents. A similar fear caused the people of Cyrene and Barca to follow their example, Cambyses graciously accepted what the Libyans sent him; the offering from Cyrene, on the contrary, he treated with contempt. I suppose he objected to the smallness of the amount – it was only 500 *minae* of silver; anyway, he snatched the money into his own hands and flung it to his men.

Ten days passed, and Cambyses, wishing to see what stuff the Egyptian king Psammenitus was made of – he had been but six months on the throne – forced him, with other Egyptians, to witness from a seat in the city outskirts a spectacle deliberately devised to humiliate him. First, he had his daughter dressed like a slave and sent out with a pitcher to fetch water, accompanied by other young girls similarly dressed and chosen from noble families. The girls cried bitterly as they passed the place where their fathers sat watching them, and the fathers, in their turn – all but Psammenitus himself – wept and lamented no less bitterly at the sight of such an insult to their children. Psammenitus, however, after a single glance of recognition, bent to the ground in silence. The girls with their pitchers passed on, and then came the king's son with two thousand others of the same age, their mouths bridled and a rope round their necks, on their way to execution for the murder of the Mytileneans at Memphis and the destruction of the ship – for the sentence of the royal judges had been that for each man ten Egyptian noblemen should die. Psammenitus watched them pass, and knew that his son was going to his death; but, though the other Egyptians who were sitting near him continued to weep and to show every sign of distress, he did just what he had done before at the sight of his daughter. So the young men, too, passed on; and then there chanced to walk by the place where Psammenitus, son of Amasis, sat with the others in the city outskirts, an old man who had once been the king's friend and had dined at his table, but had been stripped of his fortune and was now nothing more than a beggar trying to get what he could from the soldiers. At the sight of him Psammenitus burst into tears, and called him by name, and beat his head in distress. Guards were standing near, whose duty it was to report to Cambyses exactly how Psammenitus behaved as each of the processions went by, and Cambyses was so much amazed at what he heard, that he sent a messenger to Psammenitus to ask how he could behave as he did. 'Your master Cambyses,' the messenger said, 'asks why it is, that you made no sound and shed no tear when you saw your daughter insulted and your son going to his death, yet honoured with those signs of grief a beggar who, he understands, is not even related to you.' 'Son of Cyrus,' was the answer, 'my own suffering was too great for tears, but I could not but weep for the trouble of a friend, who has fallen from great wealth and good fortune and been reduced to beggary on the threshold of old age.'

When this answer was reported, it was recognized as just, and the Egyptians relate that Croesus – who, as it happened, had accompanied Cambyses in the expedition against Egypt – wept when he heard it, as did the Persians who were present, and that even Cambyses felt a touch of pity – for he at once gave orders that Psammenitus' son should be reprieved from the sentence of death, and that Psammenitus himself should be brought before him from the place where he sat in the city outskirts.

The messengers were too late to save the young man, for he had been the first to be killed; but they brought Psammenitus to Cambyses, at whose court he lived from that time onward. Here he was well treated; and indeed, if he had only had the sense to keep out of mischief, he might have recovered Egypt and ruled it as governor; for the Persians are in the habit of treating the sons of kings with honour, and even of restoring to their sons the thrones of those who have rebelled against them. There are many instances from which one may infer that this sort of generosity is usual in Persia: one obvious one is the case of Thannyras, the son of Inarus the Libyan, who was allowed to succeed his father. Pausiris, the son of Amyrtaeus, is another example: to him, too, his father's kingdom was restored – and all this in spite of the fact that nobody ever caused the Persians more trouble and loss than Inarus and Amyrtaeus. Psammenitus, however, did not refrain from stirring up trouble, and paid for it. He was caught trying to raise a revolt amongst the Egyptians, and as soon as his guilt was known by Cambyses, he drank bull's blood and died on the spot. And that was the end of Psammenitus.

Cambyses now left Memphis and went on to Sais, fully resolved on what he would do when he got there. This intention he at once carried out, for no sooner had he entered the palace of Amasis than he gave orders for his body to be taken from the tomb where it lay. This done, he proceeded to have it treated with every possible indignity, such as lashing with whips, pricking with goads, and the plucking of its hairs. All this was done till the executioners were weary, and at last, as the corpse had been embalmed and would not fall to pieces under the blows, Cambyses ordered it to be burnt. This was an unholy thing to do, because the Persians believe that fire is a god, and never burn their dead. Indeed, such a practice is unheard of either amongst them or the Egyptians: in the former case for the reason I mentioned, and because the Persians think it is wrong to give a man's dead body to a god; in the latter, because the Egyptians believe fire to be a living animal which devours whatever it gets, and, when it has eaten enough, dies with the food it feeds on. It is wholly contrary to Egyptian custom to allow dead bodies to be eaten by animals: that is why they embalm them – to prevent them from being eaten in the grave by worms. Cambyses, therefore, in giving this order, was running counter to the religious belief of both nations. The Egyptians have a story that it was not Amasis at all whose body received this treatment; it was another man's, of about the same stature, but the Persians thought it was the king's when they committed the outrage upon it. For Amasis, according to this story, had learnt from an oracle of the fate which threatened him after his death, and, in order to avert it, buried close to the doors, just within his tomb, the body of this man who was lashed with the Persian whips, but his own body he instructed his son to place in the furthest possible recess of the burial-chamber. I do not myself believe that Amasis ever gave these orders at all – it is just a tale the Egyptians tell to save face.

Cambyses next made plans for three separate military ventures: one against the Carthaginians, another against the Ammonians, and the third against the long-lived Ethiopians, on the coast of the Indian Ocean, south of Libya. He proposed to send his fleet against the Carthaginians and a part of his land forces against the Ammonians; to Ethiopia he decided first to send spies, ostensibly with presents to the king, but actually to collect what information they could; in particular he wanted them to find out if the so-called Table of the Sun really existed. (The story about the Table of the Sun is that there is a meadow, situated in the outskirts of the city, where a plentiful supply of boiled meat of all kinds is kept; it is the duty of the magistrates to put the meat there at night, and during the day anybody who wishes may come and eat it. The natives say that the meat appears spontaneously and is the gift of the earth.)

Having decided that the spies should go, Cambyses sent to Elephantine for some men of the Fish-Eaters who were acquainted with the Ethiopian language, and, while they were being fetched, gave orders for the fleet to sail against Carthage. The Phoenicians, however, refused to go, because of the close bond which connected Phoenicia and Carthage, and the wickedness of making war against their own children. In this way, with the Phoenicians out of it and the remainder of the naval force too weak to undertake the campaign alone, the Carthaginians escaped Persian domination. Cambyses did not think fit to bring pressure to bear, because the Phoenicians had taken service under him of their own free will, and his whole naval power was dependent on them. The Cyprians, too, had given their services to Persia and took part in the Egyptian campaign.

The Fish-Eaters who had been summoned from Elephantine were sent off to Ethiopia with instructions on what they were to say on their arrival: they took with them as presents for the king a scarlet robe, a gold chain-necklace and bracelets, an alabaster casket of myrrh, and a jar of palm-wine. The Ethiopians, who were the objects of all this attention, are said to be the tallest and best-looking people in the world. Their laws and customs are peculiar to themselves, and the strangest is the method they have of choosing for their king the man whom they judge to be the tallest, and strong in proportion to his height. The Fish-Eaters duly arrived in the country and presented their gifts to the king with the following words: 'Cambyses, King of Persia, wishing to be your friend and guest, has sent us here with orders to have speech with you, and these gifts he offers you are just the things which he himself takes most pleasure in using.'

But the Ethiopian king knew the men were spies, and answered: 'The king of Persia has not sent you with these presents because he puts a high value upon being my friend. You have come to get information about my kingdom; therefore, you are liars, and that king of yours is unjust. Had he any respect for what is right, he would not have coveted any other kingdom than his own, nor made slaves of a people who have done him no wrong. So take him this bow, and tell him that the king of Ethiopia has some advice to give him: when the Persians can draw a bow of this size thus easily, then let him raise an army of superior strength and invade the country of the long-lived Ethiopians. Till then, let him thank the gods for not turning the thoughts of the children of Ethiopia to foreign conquest.' He then unstrung the bow, put it into the hands of the Fish-Eaters, and picked up the scarlet robe, asking what it was and how it was made. The men explained about the dye and how the material was dipped in it, whereupon the king replied that both the dyers and the garments they dyed were pretending to be what they were not, and were therefore cheats. Then he asked about the gold chain and the bracelets, and when the Fish-Eaters explained their use as ornaments he laughed and, supposing them to be fetters, remarked that they had stronger ones in their own country. Next he asked about the myrrh, and after hearing how it was prepared and how people rubbed it on their bodies for a perfume, he repeated the comment he had made about the scarlet robe. Finally he came to the wine and, having learnt the process of its manufacture, drank some and found it delicious: then, for a last question, he asked what the Persian king ate and what was the greatest age that Persians could attain. Getting in reply an account of the nature and cultivation of wheat, and hearing that the Persian king ate bread, and that people in Persia did not commonly live beyond eighty, he said he was not surprised that anyone who ate dung should die so soon, adding that Persians would doubtless die younger still, if they did not keep themselves going with that drink – and here he pointed to the wine, the one thing in which he admitted the superiority of the Persians.

The Fish-Eaters, in their turn, asked the king how long the Ethiopians lived and what they ate, and were told that most of them lived to be a hundred and twenty, and some even more, and that they ate boiled meat and drank milk. When they expressed amazement that anyone should live to such an advanced age, they were taken to a spring, the water from which smelt like violets and caused a man's skin, when he washed in it, to glisten as if he had washed in oil. They said the water of this spring lacked density to such a degree that nothing would float in it, neither wood nor any lighter substance – everything sank to the bottom. If this account is true, then their constant use of it must be the cause of the Ethiopians' longevity. After the visit to the spring the king conducted them to a prison in which all the prisoners were bound with gold chains – for in Ethiopia the rarest and most precious metal is bronze. Inspection of the prison was followed by inspection of the Table of the Sun, and last of all they were taken to see the coffins. These coffins are said to be made of crystal, and the method the Ethiopians follow is first to dry the corpse, either by the Egyptian process or some other, then cover it all over with gypsum and paint it to resemble as closely as possible the living man; then they enclose it in a shaft of crystal which has been hollowed out, like a cylinder, to receive it. The stuff is easily worked and is mined in large quantities. The corpse is plainly visible inside the cylinder; there is no disagreeable smell, or any other cause of annoyance, and every detail can be as distinctly seen as if there were nothing between one's eyes and the body. The next-of-kin keep the cylinder in their houses for a year, offering it the first fruits and sacrificing to it; then they carry it out and set it up near the town.

Having now seen all they could, the spies returned to Egypt to make their report, which so angered Cambyses that he at once began his march against Ethiopia, without any orders for the provision of supplies, and without for a moment considering the fact that he was to take his men to the ends of the earth. He lost his wits completely and, like the madman he was, the moment he heard what the Fish-Eaters had to say, off he went with his whole force of infantry, leaving behind the Greeks who were serving under him. Arrived at Thebes, he detached a body of 50,000 men with orders to attack the Ammonians, reduce them to slavery, and burn the oracle of Zeus; then with his remaining forces he continued his march towards Ethiopia. They had not, however, covered a fifth of the distance, when everything in the nature of provisions gave out, and the men were forced to eat the pack-animals until they, too, were all gone. If Cambyses, when he saw what the situation was, had changed his mind and returned to his base, he would, in spite of his original error, have shown some sense;

but as it was, he paid not the least attention to what was happening and continued his advance. The troops kept themselves alive by eating grass so long as there was any to be had in the country, but once they had reached the desert, some of them were reduced to the dreadful expedient of cannibalism. One man in ten was chosen by lot to be the victim. This was too much even for Cambyses; when it was reported to him, he abandoned the expedition, marched back, and arrived at Thebes with greatly reduced numbers. From Thebes he went down to Memphis and allowed the Greeks to sail home. So ended the expedition against Ethiopia.

The force which was sent against the Ammonians started from Thebes with guides, and can be traced as far as the town of Oasis, which belongs to Samians supposed to be of the Aeschrionian tribe, and is seven days' journey across the sand from Thebes. The place is known in Greek as the Islands of the Blessed. General report has it that the army got as far as this, but of its subsequent fate there is no news whatever. It never reached the Ammonians and it never returned to Egypt. There is, however, a story told by the Ammonians themselves and by others who heard it from them, that when the men had left Oasis, and in their march across the desert had reached a point about mid-way between the town and the Ammonian border, a southerly wind of extreme violence drove the sand over them in heaps as they were taking their mid-day meal, so that they disappeared for ever.

After the arrival of Cambyses at Memphis, Apis – the Greek Epaphus – appeared to the Egyptians.

Immediately the whole people put on their best clothes and went on holiday, and Cambyses, seeing the festivities and convinced that the Egyptians were rejoicing over recent disaster, summoned the officers in charge of Memphis and asked them why it was that the Egyptians had done nothing of the kind during his previous visit to the city, but had waited to celebrate their holiday until the present occasion, when he had returned after the loss of a large part of his army. They replied that a god had appeared amongst them; he was wont to reveal himself only at long intervals of time, and whenever he did so, all Egypt rejoiced and celebrated a festival. Cambyses' answer to this was, that the men were liars, and as such he had them executed. Then he called the priests into his presence, and when they made precisely the same assertion, he replied that if some tame god or other had really revealed himself to the Egyptians he would find out about it soon enough; and without another word he ordered the priests to fetch Apis – which they did.

This Apis – or Epaphus – is the calf of a cow which is never afterwards able to have another. The Egyptians say that a flash of light descends upon the cow from heaven, and this causes her to receive Apis. The Apis-calf has distinctive marks: it is black, with a white diamond on its forehead, the image of an eagle on its back, the hairs on its tail double, and a scarab under its tongue. The priests brought the animal and Cambyses, half mad as he was, drew his dagger, aimed a blow at Apis' belly, but missed and struck his thigh. Then he laughed, and said to the priests: 'Do you call that a god, you poor creatures? Are your gods flesh and blood? Do they feel the prick of steel? No doubt a god like that is good enough for the Egyptians; but you won't get away with trying to make a fool of me.' He then ordered the priests to be whipped by the men whose business it was to carry out such punishments, and any Egyptian who was found still keeping holiday to be put to death. In this way the festival was broken up, the priests punished, and Apis, who lay in the temple for a time wasting away from the wound in his thigh, finally died and was buried by the priests without the knowledge of Cambyses.

Even before this Cambyses had been far from sound in his mind; but the Egyptians are convinced that the complete loss of his reason was the direct result of this crime. Of the outrages he subsequently committed the first was the murder of his brother Smerdis (his father's son by the same mother as himself). He had already sent Smerdis back to Persia, because he was jealous of him for being the only Persian to succeed in drawing – though only a very little way, about two fingers' breadth – the bow which the Fish-Eaters brought from Ethiopia. After Smerdis had returned, Cambyses dreamt that a messenger came to him from Persia with the news that Smerdis was sitting on the royal throne and that his head touched the sky. In alarm lest the dream should mean that his brother would kill him and reign in his stead, Cambyses sent Prexaspes, the most trusted of his Persian friends, to make away with him. Prexaspes went up-country to Susa and did the deed – according to one account he took his victim out hunting, according to another he lured him down to the Persian Gulf and drowned him. This, they say, was the beginning; and the next crime Cambyses committed was the murder of his sister who had come with him to Egypt. This woman was his sister by both parents, and also his wife, though it had never before been a Persian custom for brothers and sisters to marry. Cambyses got over the difficulty in the following way: having fallen in love with one of his sisters and wishing afterwards to take the illegal step of making her his wife, he summoned the royal judges and asked them if there was any law in the country which allowed a man to marry his sister if he wished to do so. These royal judges are specially chosen men, who hold office either for life or until they are found guilty of some misconduct; their duties are to determine suits and to interpret the ancient laws of the land, and all points of dispute are referred to them. When, therefore, Cambyses put his question, they managed to find an answer which would neither violate the truth nor endanger their own necks: namely, that though they could discover no law which allowed brother to marry sister, there was undoubtedly a law which permitted the king of Persia to do what he pleased. In this way they avoided breaking any established law, in spite of their fear of Cambyses; and at the same time, by bringing in a particular law to help the king to realize his wish, they escaped the danger to themselves which a too rigid attention to ancestral usage would have involved. Cambyses accordingly married the sister he was in love with, and not long afterwards married another one as well – and this, the younger of the two, was the one who went with him to Egypt.

As in the case of Smerdis, there are two accounts of her death; the Greeks say that Cambyses set a puppy and a lion-cub to fight, and that his wife was amongst the spectators; the puppy was getting the worst of it, when another from the same litter broke its chain and came to its brother's help, and the two together proved too much for the cub. Cambyses enjoyed watching the fight, but his sister, who was sitting beside him, began to cry. Noticing her tears, Cambyses asked the reason for them, and she replied that it was the sight of the puppy coming to help its brother that had made her weep; for she could not but remember Smerdis, and think how there was nobody now to come to help her husband. It was this remark which, according to the Greek version, made Cambyses put her to death. The Egyptians, on the other hand, say that the two were sitting at table, when the woman took a lettuce and, after pulling off the leaves, asked her husband whether he thought it looked better with its leaves on or off. Cambyses said that he preferred it before it was stripped, whereupon his sister replied that he had treated the house of Cyrus just as she had treated the lettuce – he had stripped it bare. Cambyses, in a fury, kicked her; and, as she was pregnant at the time, she had a miscarriage and died.

These two crimes were committed against his own kin; both were the acts of a madman – whether or not his madness was due to his treatment of Apis. It may, indeed, have been the result of any one of the many maladies which afflict mankind, and there is, in fact, a story that he had suffered from birth from the serious complaint which some call 'the sacred sickness'. There would then be nothing strange in the fact that a serious physical malady should have affected his brain. But in addition to the two crimes already mentioned, there were other Persians, too, whom he treated with the savagery of a lunatic; for instance, there was the case of Prexaspes, a man who was highly valued by the king and used to bring him his dispatches, and whose son was the king's cupbearer – also a position of no small honour. On one occasion Cambyses said to this distinguished official: 'What sort of man do the Persians think I am, and what do they say about me?' 'Master,' Prexaspes replied, 'you are highly praised by them, and they have but one criticism to make: they say you are too fond of wine.' This enraged Cambyses. 'So now,' he said, 'the Persians say that excessive drinking has driven me mad. They said something quite different before; but I see it was a lie.' For on a former occasion, when a number of Persians were sitting with him, and Croesus was also present, he had asked what they thought of him compared with his father, and they had answered that he was better than his father, because he had kept all Cyrus' possessions and acquired Egypt and the command of the sea into the bargain. Croesus, however, was not satisfied with this opinion, and said: 'Son of Cyrus, I at least do not think you are equal to your father; for you have not yet a son like the son he left behind him in yourself.' Cambyses was delighted with this, and praised Croesus' judgement, and it was the memory of this incident which made him, on the present occasion, say in a rage to Prexaspes: 'I'll soon show you if the Persians speak the truth, or if what they say is not a sign of their own madness rather than of mine. You see your son standing there by the door? If I shoot him through the middle of the heart, I shall have proved the Persians' words empty and meaningless; if I miss, then say, if you will, that the Persians are right, and my wits are gone.'

Without another word he drew his bow and shot the boy, and then ordered his body to be cut open and the wound examined; and when the arrow was found to have pierced the heart, he was delighted, and said with a laugh to the boy's father: 'There's proof for you, Prexaspes, that I am sane and the Persians mad. Now tell me if you ever saw anyone else shoot so straight.'

Prexaspes knew well enough that the king's mind was unbalanced, so in fear for his own safety he answered: 'Master, I do not believe that God himself is a better marksman.' On another occasion he arrested twelve Persians of the highest rank on some trifling charge, and buried them alive, head downwards. For this action Croesus the Lydian thought fit to give him some advice. 'My lord,' he said, 'do not always act on the passionate impulse of youth. Check and control yourself. There is wisdom in forethought, and a sensible man looks to the future. If you continue too long in your present course of killing your countrymen for no sufficient cause – and of killing children too – then beware lest the Persians rise in revolt. Again and again

your father Cyrus urged me to give you whatever advice
I might think would help you.'

In spite of the fact that Croesus spoke in all friendship, Cambyses answered: 'So even you dare tell me
how I ought to behave! You – who governed your own
country so finely, and gave such excellent advice to my
father to cross the Araxes and attack the Massagetae,
when all they wanted was to come over themselves and
attack us! You – who ruined yourself by your own bad
government, and ruined Cyrus simply because he took
your advice! But now you are going to pay for it – I
have long wanted an excuse to get even with you.' He
was just reaching for his bow to shoot him down, when
Croesus leapt from his seat and ran from the room.
Robbed of his shot, Cambyses sent his servants to catch
him and kill him; but they knew their master's moods
and hid him instead, so that if Cambyses changed his
mind and asked for Croesus, they would be able to
produce him and get a reward for saving his life; for
they knew they could kill him later, if the king kept to
his purpose and showed no signs of regret. And it did
in fact happen that quite soon afterwards Cambyses
missed Croesus, and his servants, as soon as they
noticed it, let him know that he was still alive. Cambyses said that he rejoiced to hear it, but the men who
saved him would not get off so lightly: he would punish
them with death – which he did.

All this may pass for a sample of the maniacal
savagery with which Cambyses treated the Persians and
his allies during his stay in Memphis; amongst other
things, he broke open ancient tombs and examined

the bodies, and even entered the temple of Hephaestus and jeered at the god's statue. This statue closely resembles the Pataici which the Phoenicians carry about on the prows of their triremes – but I should make it clearer to anyone who has never seen these, if I said it was like a pygmy. He also entered the temple of the Cabiri, which no one but the priest is allowed to do, made fun of the images there (they resemble those of Hephaestus, and are supposed to be his sons), and actually burnt them.

In view of all this, I have no doubt whatever that Cambyses was completely out of his mind; it is the only possible explanation of his assault upon, and mockery of, everything which ancient law and custom have made sacred in Egypt. For if anyone, no matter who, were given the opportunity of choosing from amongst all the nations in the world the beliefs which he thought best, he would inevitably, after careful consideration of their relative merits, choose those of his own country. Everyone without exception believes his own native customs, and the religion he was brought up in, to be the best; and that being so, it is unlikely that anyone but a madman would mock at such things. There is abundant evidence that this is the universal feeling about the ancient customs of one's country. One might recall, in particular, an account told of Darius. When he was king of Persia, he summoned the Greeks who happened to be present at his court, and asked them what they would take to eat the dead bodies of their fathers. They replied that they would not do it for any money in the world. Later, in the presence of the Greeks, and through an interpreter, so that they could understand what was said, he asked some Indians, of the tribe called Callatiae, who do in fact eat their parents' dead bodies, what they would take to burn them. They uttered a cry of horror and forbade him to mention such a dreadful thing. One can see by this what custom can do, and Pindar, in my opinion, was right when he called it 'king of all'.

[...]

Cambyses, son of Cyrus, after going out of his mind, still lingered on in Egypt; and while he was there, two brothers, who belonged to the caste of the Magi, rose in rebellion against him at home. One of them – Patizeithes – had been left by Cambyses as controller of his household during his absence, and this was the one who planned the revolt. Aware that Smerdis was dead, but that his death was concealed from all but a few of the Persians, most of whom believed that he was still alive, he took advantage of this state of affairs to make a bid for the throne. The brother, whom I have already mentioned as his confederate, bore a close resemblance to Cyrus' son Smerdis, the brother Cambyses had murdered. Besides the physical likeness, it also happened that he bore the same name. Patizeithes having persuaded this brother of his that he would successfully carry the business through, made him take his seat upon the royal throne, and then sent out a proclamation to the troops, not only throughout Persia but also in Egypt, that they should take their orders in future not from Cambyses but from Smerdis. The proclamation was duly published; and the herald who was instructed to take it to Egypt happened to find Cambyses and his army at Ecbatana in Syria. Here he took his stand before the assembled troops and proclaimed the new order. When Cambyses got to know of it, he at once supposed that what the herald said was true and that Prexaspes, whom he had sent to Persia to get rid of Smerdis, had failed to do so, and betrayed him. He looked at Prexaspes and said: 'So that is the way you carried out my orders!'

'Master,' Prexaspes replied, 'this is a lie. Your brother Smerdis has not rebelled against you, and you will never again have cause of quarrel with him, big or little. I did what you told me to do, and buried him with my own hands. If dead men rise from their graves, you may believe, if you will, that Astyages the Mede may return to fight against you; but if the course of nature continues unchanged, I can promise you that from Smerdis at least you will never have anything more to fear. My advice to you is, that we catch this herald and examine him, to find out who it was that sent him with this order to obey King Smerdis.'

Cambyses agreed, and a party was at once sent in pursuit of the herald. When he was brought in, Prexaspes said to him: 'You claim to have come with a message from Smerdis the son of Cyrus; now, my good fellow, if you want to get away safe, you had better tell us the truth – did Smerdis in person give you these orders, or was it one of his subordinates?'

'Since King Cambyses went with the army to Egypt,'

the man replied, 'I have never set eyes upon Smerdis the son of Cyrus. It was the Magus, whom Cambyses made steward of his household, who gave me my instructions; but he said it was on the authority of Smerdis that I was to give the message which I have.' This statement was perfectly true. Cambyses then said: 'Prexaspes, you have carried out my orders like an honest man, and no blame attaches to you; but tell me – who can it be who has assumed Smerdis' name and risen in revolt against me?'

'I think, my lord,' he replied, 'that I understand what has happened: the rebels are the two Magi – Patizeithes, whom you left in control of your household, and his brother Smerdis.'

The moment Cambyses heard the name, he was struck with the truth of what Prexaspes had said, and realized that his dream of how somebody told him that Smerdis was sitting on the throne with his head touching the sky, had been fulfilled. It was clear to him now that the murder of his brother had been all to no purpose; he lamented his loss, and at last, in bitterness and anger at the whole miserable set of circumstances, he leapt upon his horse, meaning to march with all speed to Susa and attack the Magus. But as he was springing into the saddle, the cap fell off the sheath of his sword, exposing the blade, which pierced his thigh – just in the spot where he had previously struck Apis the sacred Egyptian bull. Believing the wound to be mortal, Cambyses asked what the name of the town was, and was told it was Ecbatana. There had been a prophecy from the oracle at Buto that he would die at

Ecbatana; and he had supposed that to mean the Median Ecbatana, his capital city, where he would die in old age. But, as it turned out, the oracle meant Ecbatana in Syria. After the mention of the name, the double shock of his wound and of Patizeithes' rebellion brought him back to his senses. The meaning of the oracle became clear, and he said: 'Here it is fated that Cambyses, son of Cyrus, should die.' At the moment he said nothing more; but some twenty days later he sent for the leading Persians who were present with the army and addressed them in the following words: 'Men of Persia, circumstances compel me to reveal to you something which I have done my utmost to conceal. When I was in Egypt I had a dream – and would that I had never dreamt it! The dream was, that a messenger from Persia came to tell me that Smerdis was sitting on my throne and that his head touched the sky. Fearing my brother would rob me of the crown, I acted with more haste than judgement – for I now realize that it is not in human power to avert what is destined to be. In my folly I sent Prexaspes to Susa to kill Smerdis. The dreadful deed was done, and I lived without fear, never imagining that when Smerdis was dead another man would rise against me. Failing to grasp the true nature of what was in store for me, I murdered my brother for nothing, and have lost my kingdom just the same. It was Smerdis the Magus, not my brother, of whose rebellion God warned me in my dream. Well – I did the deed, and you may be sure you will never see Smerdis the son of Cyrus again. You have the two Magi to rule you now: Patizeithes, whom

I left in control of my household, and his brother Smerdis. The one man who of all others should have helped me against the shameful plot of the two Magi, has come to a horrid end at the hands of those nearest and dearest to him. But since he is dead, I must do that next best thing and tell you with my last breath what I would wish you to do. In the name of the gods who watch over our royal house, the command I lay upon all of you, and especially upon those of the Achaemenidae who are here present, is this: do not allow the dominion to pass again into the hands of the Medes. If they have won it by treachery, with the same weapon take it from them; if by force, then play the man and by force recover it. If you do as I bid you, I pray that the earth may be fruitful for you, your wives bear you children, your flocks multiply and freedom be yours for ever: but if you fail to recover, or make no attempt to recover, the sovereign power, then my curse be upon you – may your fate be just the opposite, and, in addition to that, may every Persian perish as miserably as I.' Having said this, Cambyses bitterly lamented the cruelty of his lot, and when the Persians saw the king in tears, they tore their clothes, and showed their sympathy by a great deal of crying and groaning. Shortly afterwards gangrene and mortification of the thigh set in, and Cambyses died, after a reign in all of seven years and five months. He had no children, either sons or daughters.

The Persians who were with Cambyses at his death found it difficult to believe that the Magi had seized power; it seemed to them much more likely that

Cambyses' story about the death of Smerdis was a malicious invention designed to set the whole of Persia against him. They were convinced that it was Smerdis the son of Cyrus who was on the throne – and all the more so because Prexaspes vehemently denied the murder, knowing, as he did, that it would be dangerous, now that Cambyses was gone, to admit that a son of Cyrus had died by his hand. The result was that the Magus, after assuming the name of Smerdis, son of Cyrus, found himself securely on the throne, and continued there for the seven months which were needed to make up the eighth year of Cambyses. During this time his subjects received great benefits from him, and he was regretted after his death by all the Asiatics under his rule, except by the Persians themselves, for to every nation within his dominion he proclaimed, directly he came to the throne, a three years' remission of taxes and military service. But after seven months of power, the following circumstances led to his exposure.

The first person to suspect that he was not the son of Cyrus, but an impostor, was a certain Otanes, the son of Pharnaspes, one of the wealthiest members of the Persian nobility, and his suspicions were aroused by the fact that Smerdis never ventured outside the central fortifications of the capital, and never summoned any eminent Persians to a private audience.

Now when the Magus usurped the throne, he took over all Cambyses' wives, amongst whom there was a daughter of Otanes called Phaidime. Otanes, to test the truth of his suspicions, sent a message to this daughter, and asked her who it was she slept with – Smerdis the son of Cyrus, or some other man. She replied that she did not know; she had never seen Smerdis the son of Cyrus, and had no idea who her husband was. Otanes sent a second message: 'If,' it ran, 'you do not yourself know Smerdis the son of Cyrus, ask Atossa who it is with whom you both live. She can hardly fail to know her own brother.' Phaidime replied: 'I have no means of speaking to Atossa, nor of seeing any other of the king's wives; for as soon as this man, whoever he may be, came to the throne, he separated us and gave us all different quarters.' This was a further indication of the truth of what Otanes suspected, so he sent a third message to his daughter. 'Phaidime,' he wrote, 'you have noble blood in your veins, and must not shrink from any danger your father orders you to face. If your husband is the man I think he is, and not the son of Cyrus, he must not get away with sharing your bed and sitting on the throne of Persia. He must be punished. This, then, is what you must do: next time he spends the night with you, wait till you are sure he is asleep and then feel for his ears. If you find that he has got ears, consider yourself the wife of Smerdis, son of Cyrus; but if he has none, then you will know you are married to Smerdis the Magus.' Phaidime answered that it would be an extremely risky thing to do; for if her husband proved to have no ears, and she were caught feeling for them, he would be certain to kill her. Nevertheless she was willing to take the risk. Now when Cyrus was on the throne he had punished Smerdis the Magus for some serious crime by having his ears cut off.

Phaidime, then, kept the promise she had made to her father Otanes; when her turn came to sleep with the Magus (in Persia a man's wives share his bed in rotation), she entered the bedroom, lay down, and then, as soon as the Magus was soundly asleep, felt for his ears. She quickly satisfied herself that he had not got any; so next morning she lost no time in letting her father know the result of the experiment. Otanes took into his confidence Aspathines and Gobryas, two eminent Persians whom he had special reason to trust, and told them of his discovery. Both these men already had their suspicions of the truth, and were ready enough, in consequence, to accept what Otanes said, and it was then agreed that each of the three should choose his most trustworthy friend and bring him in as an accomplice. Otanes chose Intaphrenes, Gobryas Megabyzus, and Aspathines Hydarnes. The number of conspirators was thus raised to six, and on the arrival at Susa from Persia of Darius, whose father Hystaspes was governor there, it was decided to add him to the number.

The seven conspirators now met to pledge loyalty to one another and discuss the measures they were to take. When it was Darius' turn to express his views, he said that he had supposed himself to be the only person who knew that Smerdis the son of Cyrus was dead, and that the present king was the Magus. 'And for that very reason,' he went on, 'I hurried to Susa in order to arrange to get rid of him. Now, as it turns out that I am not the only one in the secret, my opinion is that we should act promptly. There would be nothing but danger in delay.'

Otanes answered: 'You are the son of Hystaspes, Darius, and seem likely to prove as good a man as he; nevertheless I advise you not to be rash or in too much of a hurry. What we need is prudence – and we must add to our number before we strike the blow.'

'Listen, all of you,' Darius replied; 'if you take Otanes' advice, the result will be ruin for everyone. Somebody is sure to seek advantage for himself by betraying us to the Magus. You ought really to have done this thing entirely on your own; but as you have seen fit to let others in on it, and have communicated your intentions to me, I have only one thing to say – let us act immediately. If we let a single day slip by, I promise you one thing: nobody will have time to betray *me* – for I will myself denounce you all to the Magus.'

Otanes was alarmed by the passionate urgency of Darius. 'I see,' he said, 'that you are determined to compel us to rush, and will not allow us a moment's delay for deliberation. But can you tell us how to get into the palace to make our attack? Doubtless you know as well as we do that there are guards everywhere; even if you haven't seen them, you have surely heard of them. How are we to get past?'

'Otanes,' Darius answered, 'there are many occasions when words are useless, and only deeds will make a man's meaning plain; often enough, too, it is easy to talk – and only to talk, for no brave act follows. You know there will be no difficulty in passing the guards.

Who will dare to refuse admission to men of our rank and distinction, if not from respect, then from fear of the consequences? Besides, I have a perfect excuse for getting us in: I will say I have just come from Persia and have a message from my father for the king. If a lie is necessary, why not speak it? We are all after the same thing, whether we lie or speak the truth: our own advantage. Men lie when they think to profit by deception, and tell the truth for the same reason – to get something they want, and to be the better trusted for their honesty. It is only two different roads to the same goal. Were there no question of advantage, the honest man would be as likely to lie as the liar is, and the liar would tell the truth as readily as the honest man. Any sentry who lets us through without question, will be rewarded later; anyone who tries to stop us must be treated instantly as an enemy. We must force our way past him and set to work at once.'

'Friends,' said Gobryas, 'will there ever be a better moment than now to save the throne – or, if we fail, to die in the attempt? Are Persians to be ruled by a Mede – a Magus – a fellow who has had his ears chopped off? Those of you who stood by the deathbed of Cambyses are not likely to forget his dying curse upon the Persians who should make no effort to save the throne. We took it lightly then – thinking Cambyses was speaking slander. But now the situation has changed, and I propose that we follow Darius' advice, and break up the meeting for no other purpose than to march straight to the palace and attack the Magus.' All the conspirators agreed to this proposal.

While this discussion was in progress, events had been taking place elsewhere. The two Magi had been thinking things over and had decided to take Prexaspes into their confidence. There were several reasons for this decision: first, Prexaspes had been cruelly treated by Cambyses, who shot his son dead; then, as he had been directly responsible for the murder of Smerdis the son of Cyrus, he was the only person in the secret of his death; and, lastly, he was highly respected in Persian society. They summoned him therefore to their presence and began to bargain for his support; they tried to get from him a promise upon oath never to say a word to anybody about the hoax they had practised upon the Persians, and offered to pay him enormous sums as the price of his silence. Prexaspes agreed, whereupon the Magi made the further proposal that they should themselves call upon all the Persians to meet at the base of the palace wall, and that Prexaspes should proclaim, from the top of a tower, that the king was none other than Smerdis the son of Cyrus. In giving Prexaspes these instructions, the Magi relied on the fact that the Persians would be more likely to believe him than anyone else, seeing that he had frequently denied the murder and expressed the opinion that Smerdis was still alive. Again Prexaspes agreed; so the Magi summoned the people to assemble, and told Prexaspes to climb to the top of the tower and make his declaration. But then Prexaspes, deliberately ignoring everything which the Magi had asked him to say, made a speech in which he traced the genealogy of Cyrus right back from Achaemenes, went on to describe the great services which Cyrus had rendered to his country, and finally revealed the true state of affairs, adding that he had concealed it hitherto out of regard to his own safety, but that the time had now come when it was no longer possible to hold his tongue. He kept back nothing; he himself, he said, had been forced by Cambyses to kill Smerdis the son of Cyrus, and the country was now in the power of the two Magi. Finally, with a prayer that the Persians might suffer untold misery if they did not recover the throne and punish the usurpers, he threw himself headlong from the tower to the ground. Such was the end of Prexaspes, who throughout his life had been a man of high distinction.

Meanwhile the seven conspirators, having reached their decision to attack the Magi without a moment's delay, had prayed for luck and were on their way to the palace. They knew nothing about the affair of Prexaspes, and were half-way there before they learnt the truth. The news pulled them up, for they thought it advisable to discuss this new element in the situation. The supporters of Otanes urged delay and the risk of making their attempt until things calmed down again; but Darius and his party were still for immediate action and opposed to any change of plan. The argument was growing hot, when they suddenly saw seven pairs of hawks chasing two pairs of vultures, which they tore at, as they flew, with both beak and claw. It was an omen; forthwith the plan of Darius was unanimously accepted, and with renewed confidence the seven men hurried on towards the palace. When they reached the gates, everything turned out just as Darius had foreseen: the sentries, out of respect for their exalted rank and having no suspicion of the real purpose of their visit, allowed them to pass without question – almost as if they were under the special protection of heaven. In the great court, however, they were met by some of the eunuchs – the king's messengers – who stopped them and asked their business, at the same time threatening the guards for having let them through. The check was momentary; eager to press on, the seven, with a word of mutual encouragement, drew their daggers, stabbed the eunuchs who were trying to hold them up, and ran forward into the hall.

Both the Magi were at this time indoors, discussing the situation which had been brought about by Prexaspes' treachery. They heard the eunuchs crying out in evident alarm, and sprang up to see what the matter was; then, realizing their danger, they at once prepared to fight it out. One just had time to get his bow down, the other seized his spear. The one with the bow had no chance to use it – the fight was at much too close quarters; the other, however, used his spear to advantage, keeping off his attackers and wounding Aspathines in the leg, and Intaphrenes in the eye – Intaphrenes, as a result of the wound, lost his eye but survived. His companion, unable to use his bow and finding himself defenceless, ran into a bedroom, which opened out of the hall, and tried to shut the doors on his pursuers; but two of them, Darius and Gobryas, managed to force their way in with him, and Gobryas got his arms round the Magus. It was dark in the room, and Darius, standing over the two men locked together on the floor, hesitated to intervene; for he was afraid that, if he struck, he might kill the wrong man. But Gobryas, aware of his hesitation, cried out: 'What's your hand for – if you don't use it?'

'I dare not strike,' said Darius, 'for fear of killing you.'

'Fear nothing,' answered Gobryas; 'spit both of us at once – if need be.'

Darius then drove his dagger home – by luck into the body of the Magus.

When both the Magi had been killed, the confederates decapitated them, and ran out into the street, shouting and making a great noise, with the severed heads in their hands. The two wounded men had been left behind in the palace, being too weak to move – they were needed, moreover, to keep a watch upon the citadel. Once outside, the five who were unhurt appealed to their fellow citizens, told them what had happened, and showed them the heads – and then set about murdering every Magus they came across. The other Persians, once they had learnt of the exploit of the seven confederates, and understood the hoax which the two brothers had practised on them, were soon ready to follow their example: they, too, drew their daggers and killed every Magus they could find – so that if darkness had not put an end to the slaughter, the whole tribe would have been exterminated. The anniversary of this day has become a red-letter day in the Persian calendar, marked by an important festival known as the Magophonia, or Killing of the Magi, during which no Magus is allowed to show himself –

every member of the tribe stays indoors till the day is over.

Five days later, when the excitement had died down, the conspirators met to discuss the situation in detail. At the meeting certain speeches were made – some of the Greeks refuse to believe they were actually made at all; nevertheless they were. The first speaker was Otanes, and his theme was to recommend the establishment in Persia of popular government. 'I think,' he said, 'that the time has passed for any one man amongst us to have absolute power. Monarchy is neither pleasant nor good. You know to what lengths the pride of power carried Cambyses, and you have personal experience of the effect of the same thing in the conduct of the Magus. How can one fit monarchy into any sound system of ethics, when it allows a man to do whatever he likes without any responsibility or control? Even the best of men raised to such a position would be bound to change for the worse – he could not possibly see things as he used to do. The typical vices of a monarch are envy and pride; envy, because it is a natural human weakness, and pride, because excessive wealth and power lead to the delusion that he is something more than a man. These two vices are the root cause of all wickedness: both lead to acts of savage and unnatural violence. Absolute power ought, by rights, to preclude envy on the principle that the man who possesses it has also at command everything he could wish for; but in fact it is not so, as the behaviour of kings to their subjects proves: they are jealous of the best of them merely for continuing to live, and take pleasure in the worst; and no one is readier than a king to listen to tale-bearers. A king, again, is the most inconsistent of men; show him reasonable respect, and he is angry because you do not abase yourself before his majesty; abase yourself, and he hates you for being a toady. But the worst of all remains to be said – he breaks up the structure of ancient tradition and law, forces women to serve his pleasure, and puts men to death without trial. Contrast with this the rule of the people: first, it has the finest of all names to describe it – equality under law; and, secondly, the people in power do none of the things that monarchs do. Under a government of the people a magistrate is appointed by lot and is held responsible for his conduct in office, and all questions are put up for open debate. For these reasons I propose that we do away with the monarchy, and raise the people to power; for the state and the people are synonymous terms.'

Otanes was followed by Megabyzus, who recommended the principle of oligarchy in the following words: 'Insofar as Otanes spoke in favour of abolishing monarchy, I agree with him; but he is wrong in asking us to transfer political power to the people. The masses are a feckless lot – nowhere will you find more ignorance or irresponsibility or violence. It would be an intolerable thing to escape the murderous caprice of a king, only to be caught by the equally wanton brutality of the rabble. A king does at least act consciously and deliberately; but the mob does not. Indeed how should it, when it has never been taught what is right and proper, and has no knowledge of its own about such things? The masses handle affairs without thought; all they can do is to rush blindly into politics like a river in flood. As for the people, then, let them govern Persia's enemies; but let us ourselves choose a certain number of the best men in the country, and give *them* political power. We personally shall be amongst them, and it is only natural to suppose that the best men will produce the best policy.'

Darius was the third to speak. 'I support,' he said, 'all Megabyzus' remarks about the masses but I do not agree with what he said of oligarchy. Take the three forms of government we are considering – democracy, oligarchy, and monarchy – and suppose each of them to be the best of its kind; I maintain that the third is greatly preferable to the other two. One ruler: it is impossible to improve upon that – provided he is the best. His judgement will be in keeping with his character; his control of the people will be beyond reproach; his measures against enemies and traitors will be kept secret more easily than under other forms of government. In an oligarchy, the fact that a number of men are competing for distinction in the public service cannot but lead to violent personal feuds; each of them wants to get to the top, and to see his own proposals carried; so they quarrel. Personal quarrels lead to civil wars, and then to bloodshed; and from that state of affairs the only way out is a return to monarchy – a clear proof that monarchy is best. Again, in a democracy, malpractices are bound to occur; in this case, however, corrupt dealings in government services lead not to private feuds, but to close personal associations, the men responsible for them putting their heads together and mutually supporting one another. And so it goes on, until somebody or other comes forward as the people's champion and breaks up the cliques which are out for their own interests. This wins him the admiration of the mob, and as a result he soon finds himself entrusted with absolute power – all of which is another proof that the best form of government is monarchy. To sum up: where did we get our freedom from, and who gave it us? Is it the result of democracy, or of oligarchy, or of monarchy? We were set free by one man, and therefore I propose that we should pre-serve that form of government, and, further, that we should refrain from changing ancient ways, which have served us well in the past. To do so would not profit us.'

These were the three views set out in the three speeches, and the four men who had not spoken voted for the last. Otanes (who had urged equality before the law), finding the decision against him, then made another speech. 'My friends,' he said, 'it is clear that the king will have to be one of ourselves, whether we draw lots for it, or ask the people of Persia to make their choice between us, or use some other method. I will not compete with you for the crown, for I have no wish to rule – or to *be* ruled either. I withdraw, there-fore, upon one condition: that neither I myself, nor any of my descendants, shall be forced to submit to the rule of that one of you, whoever he is, who becomes king.' The other six agreed to this condition, and Otanes stood down. To this day the family of Otanes continues to be the only free family in Persia, and submits to the king only so far as the members of it may choose, while not disobeying the laws of the Persians.

The other six then discussed the fairest way of deciding who should have the throne. They agreed that, if it fell to any of themselves, Otanes and his descendants should receive, every year, a suit of Median clothes and such other gifts as are held to be of most value by the Persians, as a mark of honour for the part he had played in the plot against the Magi, of which he was the prime mover and principal organizer. These privileges were for Otanes only; they also agreed upon another to be shared by all: permission, namely, for any of the seven to enter the royal presence unannounced, except when the king was in bed with a woman. They further agreed that the king should not marry outside the families of the seven confederates. To choose which should be king, they proposed to mount their horses on the outskirts of the city, and he whose horse neighed first after the sun was up should have the throne.

Darius had a clever groom called Oebares. After the meeting had broken up, he went to see this fellow, and told him of the arrangement they had come to, whereby they should sit on their horses' backs and the throne should be given to the one whose horse neighed first as the sun rose. 'So if,' he added, 'you can think of some contrivance or other, do what you can to see that this prize falls to me, and to no one else.'

'Well, master,' Oebares answered, 'if your chance of winning the throne depends upon nothing but that you may set your mind at rest; you may be perfectly confident – you, and nobody else, will be king. I know a charm which will just suit our purpose.'

'If,' said Darius, 'you really have got something which will do the trick, you had better hurry and get it all worked out, for tomorrow is the day.'

Oebares, accordingly, as soon as it was dark, took from the stables the mare which Darius' horse was particularly fond of, and tied her up on the outskirts of the city. Then he brought along the stallion and led him round and round the mare, getting closer and closer in narrowing circles, and finally allowed him to mount her. Next morning just before dawn the six men, according to their agreement, came riding on their horses through the city suburb, and when they reached the spot where the mare had been tethered on the previous night, Darius' horse started forward and neighed. At the same instant, though the sky was clear, there was a flash of lightning and a clap of thunder, as if it were a sign from heaven; the election of Darius was assured, and the other five leapt from their saddles and bowed to the ground at his feet.

That is one account of how Oebares made the horse neigh. The Persians also have another, namely that he rubbed the mare's genitals and then kept his hand covered inside his breeches. When the sun was rising and the horses were about to be released, he drew his hand out and put it to the nostrils of Darius' horse, which at the smell of the mare at once snorted and neighed.

In this way Darius son of Hystaspes became king of Persia. Following the conquests of Cyrus and Cambyses, his dominion extended over the whole of Asia, with the exception of Arabia. The Arabs had never been reduced to subjection by the Persians, but friendly relations had continued between the two countries ever since the Arabs let Cambyses pass through their territory on his Egyptian campaign; for without this service the invasion of Egypt would have been impracticable.

The first women Darius married were Cyrus' two daughters Atossa and Artystone; the former had previously been the wife of her brother Cambyses and also of the Magus; the latter was a virgin. Subsequently he married Parmys, a daughter of Cyrus' son Smerdis, and, in addition to these, the daughter of Otanes, the man who had exposed the Magus.

Now that his power was felt in every corner of his dominions, his first act was to erect a stone monument with a carving of a man on horseback, and the following inscription: *Darius, son of Hystaspes, by the virtue of his horse and of his groom Oebares, won the throne of Persia.* The horse's name was included.

[...]

There is a plain in Asia surrounded by a ring of hills, which are broken by clefts in five separate places. This tract of land used to belong to the Chorasmians and lies on the boundaries of five different tribes: the Chorasmians themselves, the Hyrcanians, the Parthians, the Sarangians, and the Thamanaeans; but ever since the Persian rise to power it has been the property of the Persian king. In the ring of hills a considerable river rises – the Aces – which used to supply water to the five tribes I have mentioned, being split into five channels and flowing out to each of them through a different gorge; now, however, that the Persians are masters of the country, all these people find themselves in a serious difficulty, for the king has blocked up the gorges and constructed sluice-gates to contain the flow of water, so that what used to be a plain has now become a large lake, the river flowing in as before but no longer having any means of egress. The result of this for the people who depended upon the use of the water, but are now deprived of it, has been disastrous. In winter, to be sure, they get rain like anyone else, but they need the river water when they are sowing their millet and sesame in the summer. When therefore they find themselves waterless, they go in a body with their wives to the Persians, and stand howling in front of the gates of the king's palace, until the king gives orders to open the sluices and allow the water to flow to whichever tribe it may be that needs it most. Then, when the land has drunk all the water it wants, the sluices are shut, and the king orders others to be opened in turn, according to the needs of the remaining tribes. I know that he opens the sluices only upon receipt of a heavy payment over and above the regular tax.

Soon after the rising of the seven Persians against the Magus, one of their number, Intaphrenes, was executed for a failure to show proper respect to the king's authority. Having business to transact with Darius, he wished to enter the palace. Now it had already been

agreed that any of the conspirators might visit the
king unannounced, provided that he was not, at the
moment, in bed with a woman; and in view of this
Intaphrenes refused to have his name sent in by a
messenger, and claimed it as his right, as one of the
seven, to walk straight in. He was, however, stopped
by the king's chamberlain and the sentry on duty at the
palace gate, who told him that Darius had, in fact, a
woman with him at the time. Thinking this was only
a trumped-up excuse to keep him out, Intaphrenes
drew his scimitar and cut off their ears and noses,
strung them on his horse's bridle, tied the bridle round
their necks, and sent them packing. They showed
themselves to Darius and explained the reason for their
plight, which at once suggested to the king the alarm-
ing possibility of a fresh conspiracy. Thinking his six
former confederates might all be in this business
together, he sent for each of them in turn, and sounded
them to see if they approved of what Intaphrenes had
done. None of them did; so as soon as he was satisfied
that Intaphrenes had acted entirely on his own initiat-
ive, he had him arrested with his children and all his
near relations, in the strong suspicion that he and his
family were about to raise a revolt. All the prisoners
were then chained, as condemned criminals. After his
arrest, Intaphrenes' wife came to the palace and began
to weep and lament outside the door, and continued
so long to do so that Darius, moved to pity by her
incessant tears, sent someone out to speak to her.
'Lady,' the message ran, 'the king is willing to spare
the life of one member of your family – choose which

of the prisoners you wish to save.' Having thought this offer over, the woman answered that, if the king granted her the life of one only of her family, she would choose her brother. The answer amazed Darius, and he sent again and asked why it was that she rejected her husband and children, and preferred to save her brother, who was neither so near to her as her children, nor so dear as her husband. 'My lord,' she replied, 'God willing, I may get another husband, and other children when these are gone. But as my father and mother are both dead, I can never possibly have another brother. That was the reason for what I said.' Darius appreciated the lady's good sense, and, to mark his pleasure, granted her not only the life she asked, but also that of her eldest son. The rest of the family were all put to death. This, then, was the early end of one of the seven confederates.

[...]

THE STORY OF PENGUIN CLASSICS

Before 1946 ...'Classics' are mainly the domain of academics and students, without readable editions for everyone else. This all changes when a little-known classicist, E. V. Rieu, presents Penguin founder Allen Lane with the translation of Homer's *Odyssey* that he has been working on and reading to his wife Nelly in his spare time.

1946 *The Odyssey* becomes the first Penguin Classic published, and promptly sells three million copies. Suddenly, classic books are no longer for the privileged few.

1950s Rieu, now series editor, turns to professional writers for the best modern, readable translations, including Dorothy L. Sayers's *Inferno* and Robert Graves's *The Twelve Caesars*, which revives the salacious original.

1960s The Classics are given the distinctive black jackets that have remained a constant throughout the series's various looks. Rieu retires in 1964, hailing the Penguin Classics list as 'the greatest educative force of the 20th century'.

1970s A new generation of translators arrives to swell the Penguin Classics ranks, and the list grows to encompass more philosophy, religion, science, history and politics.

1980s The Penguin American Library joins the Classics stable, with titles such as *The Last of the Mohicans* safeguarded. Penguin Classics now offers the most comprehensive library of world literature available.

1990s The launch of Penguin Audiobooks brings the classics to a listening audience for the first time, and in 1999 the launch of the Penguin Classics website takes them online to a larger global readership than ever before.

The 21st Century Penguin Classics are rejacketed for the first time in nearly twenty years. This world famous series now consists of more than 1300 titles, making the widest range of the best books ever written available to millions – and constantly redefining the meaning of what makes a 'classic'.

The Odyssey continues ...

The best books ever written

PENGUIN CLASSICS

SINCE 1946

Find out more at www.penguinclassics.com